T0331517

Supercell featuring Hatsune Miku

33 1/3 Global

33 1/3 Global, a series related to but independent from **33 1/3**, takes the format of the original series of short, music-based books and brings the focus to music throughout the world. With initial volumes focusing on Japanese and Brazilian music, the series will also include volumes on the popular music of Australia/Oceania, Europe, Africa, the Middle East, and more.

33 1/3 Japan

Series Editor: Noriko Manabe

Series Board: Marië Abe, Michael Bourdaghs, Shelley Brunt, Kevin Fellezs, Akitsugu Kawamoto, Yoshitaka Mōri, Dexter Thomas, Christine Yano

Spanning a range of artists and genres—from the 1960s rock of Happy End to technopop band Yellow Magic Orchestra, the Shibuya-kei of Cornelius, classic anime series *Cowboy Bebop*, J-Pop/EDM hybrid Perfume, and vocaloid star Hatsune Miku—**33 1/3 Japan** is a series devoted to in-depth examination of Japanese music of the twentieth and twenty-first centuries.

Forthcoming titles:

Yoko Kanno's *Cowboy Bebop Soundtrack* by Rose Bridges

Perfume's *Game* by Patrick St. Michel

33 1/3 Brazil

Series Editor: Jason Stanyek

Covering the genres of samba, tropicália, rock, hip hop, forró, bossa nova, heavy metal, and funk, among others, **33 1/3 Brazil** is a series devoted to in-depth examination of the most important Brazilian albums of the twentieth and twenty-first centuries.

Forthcoming titles:

Tim Maia's Tim Maia Racional Vols 1 & 2 by Allen Thayer

Caetano Veloso's *A Foreign Sound* by Barbara Browning

João Gilberto and Stan Getz's *Getz/Gilberto* by Brian McCann

Supercell featuring Hatsune Miku

Keisuke Yamada

Noriko Manabe, Series Editor

Bloomsbury Academic
An imprint of Bloomsbury Publishing Inc.

B L O O M S B U R Y
NEW YORK • LONDON • OXFORD • NEW DELHI • SYDNEY

Bloomsbury Academic
An imprint of Bloomsbury Publishing Inc.

50 Bedford Square	1385 Broadway
London	New York
WC1B 3DP	NY 10018
UK	USA

www.bloomsbury.com

BLOOMSBURY and the Diana logo are trademarks of Bloomsbury Publishing Plc

First published 2017

Library of Congress Cataloging-in-Publication Data
Names: Yamada, Keisuke, 1984- author.
Title: Supercell featuring Hatsune Miku / Keisuke Yamada.
Description: New York ; London : Bloomsbury Academic, 2017. | Series: 33 1/3 Japan | Includes bibliographical references and index.
Identifiers: LCCN 2017002966 (print) | LCCN 2017017210 (ebook) | ISBN 9781501325960 (ePDF) | ISBN 9781501325946 (ePUB) | ISBN 9781501325977 (pbk.   )
Subjects: LCSH: Electronica (Music)--Social aspects–Japan–History–21st century. | Electronica (Music)--Japan–History and criticism. | Hatsune, Miku (Fictional character) | Supercell (Musical group). Supercell. | Vocaloid (Computer file) | Voice synthesizers.
Classification: LCC ML3917.J3 (ebook) | LCC ML3917.J3 Y36 2017 (print) | DDC 782.421648092/2–dc23
LC record available at https://lccn.loc.gov/2017002966

ISBN:	HB:	978-1-5013-2598-4
	PB:	978-1-5013-2597-7
	ePub:	978-1-5013-2594-6
	ePDF:	978-1-5013-2596-0

Series: 33 $\frac{1}{3}$ Japan

Cover image © jericho667/Getty images

Typeset in the U.K. by Fakenham Prepress Solutions, Fakenham, Norfolk NR21 8NN

To the memory of Sachiko

Contents

Acknowledgments

I would like to express my gratitude to mentors and colleagues who have made writing this book truly a delightful and precious experience. I would particularly like to thank Jim Sykes for his insightful comments and suggestions on the earlier version of the manuscript. I wish to thank Christine Yano for her helpful suggestions on the manuscript and for her encouragement. I also appreciate constructive suggestions provided by an anonymous reader. I am grateful to Leah Babb-Rosenfeld, Susan Krogulski, and the entire production staff at Bloomsbury for their careful attention to the project. Special thanks are due to the Series Editor for **33 1/3 Japan,** and my mentor, Noriko Manabe, for her critical reading of the manuscript, for her thoughtful suggestions, and for guiding me at every stage of the project.

Notes on Japanese Names and Translations

When Japanese names appear in the text, the surname comes before the given name, per standard usage in Japan, except for those of authors of scholarly articles or books originally written in English. All translations from Japanese are my own, with the exception of those already available in English.

Introduction

It all started by posting videos by myself, through the Nico Nico Douga video sharing site. I gradually gathered illustrators and designers together. In Japan there is a large annual event called Comic Market [Comiket] and I started to create songs to participate in this event. Matching up music and the illustrations and composing songs gave birth to [S]upercell … I probably would have ended up just making music for my [own] satisfaction, but the web definitely brought my music to a wider audience. **RYO 2011**

This excerpt from an interview with Ryo, composer and lyricist of the eleven-piece creator group[1] Supercell, was originally posted on the web forum of the Anime News Network on June 21, 2011. It was eleven days before Japanese pop star Hatsune Miku would give her US debut concert at the Nokia Theatre L.A. LIVE (now Microsoft Theater) in Los Angeles. Accompanied by a live band with keyboards, electric guitar, bass, drums, strings, and other instrumentalists, Miku performed twenty-seven songs, thrilling the American audience. None of this would seem surprising, as the show was part of Anime Expo—North America's largest annual event for anime and manga, the Japanese animation and comics that have gained a loyal, even fanatical, following. Given that many in the audience were fans of Japanese pop culture, the enthusiastic reception was not at all that surprising—except that *Miku isn't physically human*:

she is a virtual character, a Vocaloid (synthesizer of the singing voice) invented by Crypton Future Media. Her performance was holographic, and her voice was produced by Yamaha's Vocaloid technology, which VocaloPs (Vocaloid producers) had programmed.[2] One of the songs Miku performed that night was Ryo's song, "The World Is Mine," from *Supercell* (2009), his group's first album.

This book is about Ryo's creator group, Supercell, and its eponymous first album, which features Hatsune Miku, as well as cultural contexts that supported circulation of its works and enhanced its visibility in musical communities. The group consists of eleven members: Ryo as composer, lyricist, and band leader, along with ten other visual artists, designers, and their supporters, who provide illustrations and designs for the group's music videos, album cases, and booklets. The album *Supercell* was released in Japan on March 4, 2009, by Sony Music Japan, one of Japan's leading record companies. Ryo composed all of its twelve musical pieces with *Hatsune Miku* software, which was released in August 2007. By the end of 2007, Ryo had already composed several Vocaloid songs. At that point, Ryo says, he was "just making music for [his own] satisfaction," rather than making Vocaloid works as his profession. These Vocaloid works, then, were not primarily— or at least were not originally—designed to be performed in front of large audiences. Rather, they developed as part of so-called DTM (desktop music) culture, in which composers utilize computer software and digital synthesizers for making music at home, and which has facilitated Japanese amateur music-making scenes since the late 1980s. The DTM culture that emerged since the late 2000s, however, has turned out to be quite distinct from that of the 1980s. There are fundamental questions regarding the developmental process of

DTM culture that need to be addressed: What cultural and social factors—what I will call "settings"—helped DTM culture, as practiced by bedroom hobbyists like Ryo, to flourish? What allowed these creators to bring their music to a wider global audience, as illustrated by Hatsune Miku's live performances at the 2011 Anime Expo, Japan Expo, or Fan Expo Canada? What does this practice say about the development of music technology and human–technology interactions?

One of the settings is the voice synthesis software *Hatsune Miku*. This software combines the 2D character Hatsune Miku, as designed by Japanese illustrator KEI, with a database of voice samples—or "singer library"—of Japanese voice actress Fujita Saki (Figure 1). The technology enables users to feel as if they are pop idol producers, as the Vocaloid character sings whatever a composer creates with the software. Furthermore, it motivates some consumers to create what Japanese cultural critic Azuma Hiroki (2009) calls "derivative works"—a rereading and reproduction of the original, in this case, a consumer's own illustration of the Vocaloid character rather than the *original* design by KEI. As Azuma writes, "depending on the differing modes of 'reading up' by users, consumers … can produce any number of derivative works that differ from the originals" (ibid.: 33). This is the case with Supercell, in which those artists belonging to the group provide their own derivative works of the Vocaloid character.

A second notable setting in DTM culture is online video-sharing platforms. As mentioned in the interview, Ryo began his creative activity as an *amateur* VocaloP by posting his own works on the video-sharing website Niconico (formerly known as Nico Nico Douga). Niconico has been run by media company Niwango, a subsidiary of Japanese media company Dwango, since December 2006. In addition to allowing users

Figure 1 *Hatsune Miku illustrated by KEI © Crypton Future Media, INC.*
www.piapro.net

to upload and share digital video clips, as with YouTube, Niconico offers the extra feature of allowing viewers to leave comments at specific points in the video, so that subsequent viewers of the video see them scroll across the screen. This feature gives Niconico viewers a sense of liveness and active participation that is largely absent in a YouTube playback. Ryo uploaded some of his earlier works, such as "Melt" (on December 7, 2007) and "The World Is Mine" (on May 31, 2008), on the Niconico site. Through this socially interactive space, he met artists and illustrators who would later become the members of Supercell. Japanese music journalist Shiba Tomonori (2014) calls Niconico a new "playground" (*asobi-ba*) for DTM creators.

Rather than a "place," the "playground" functions as a "space" in which to strengthen social and cultural connections among user-creators "with all kinds of objectives, goals, values, and asymmetrical power relations" (Gustavson and Cytrynbaum 2003: 256). A place is a location that people visit, occupy, and inhabit; they interact with each other in that location. A place itself is, however, passive. A space, on the other hand, is the way in which the place is used by people—and even where an environment has some sort of agency or effects on people (e.g., earthquakes and floods). As Gustavson and Cytrynbaum write, "For a place to be a space, people must be involved in the place for particular reasons over time" (2003: 256). In this sense, the Niconico site becomes a playground space when VocaloPs, illustrators, and collaborators interact with each other on the online platform over time. This highly collaborative space is an important aspect of the settings in which DTM culture is practiced.

This book explores the Vocaloid phenomena through the lenses of media and fan studies. On the one hand, Ryo is a *consumer and user* of Vocaloid software and Niconico; at the same time, he is a *producer and creator* of content of the video-sharing site through Vocaloid technology, which is available to other users of the website. Furthermore, he collaborates with other artists and illustrators in Vocaloid works. The question of how we deal with such blurred boundaries between cultural consumers and producers in the age of new media has been widely discussed in the field of media studies. In *Convergence Culture: Where Old and New Media Collide* (2006), Henry Jenkins explores the concept of participatory culture to distinguish the cultural phenomena happening around "interactive new media" from "passive old media." Jenkins writes:

> The term, participatory culture, contrasts with older notions of passive media spectatorship. Rather than talking about media producers and consumers as occupying separate roles, we might now see them as participants who interact with each other according to a new set of rules that none of us fully understands. Not all participants are created equal. Corporations—and even individuals within corporate media—still exert greater power than any individual consumer or even the aggregate of consumers. And some consumers have greater abilities to participate in this emerging culture than others.
>
> Jenkins 2006: 3

My study, however, attempts to go beyond the consumer–producer dichotomy. Rather than discussing one's economic roles in today's participatory culture, what follows focuses on the processes in which (amateur) composers, illustrators, and artists as well as the cultural products they create become visible to others, both socially and culturally. Online interactive platforms have given individuals more chances to converge and collaborate in order to produce and circulate creative works. In this sense, Niconico and Vocaloid singing synthesizer technology have enabled individual creators and their cultural products to become visible, influential, and powerful, forming a new playground for them.

This book also explores the individual agency of such enhanced creators and their capabilities to construct and expand their playground beyond cyberspace. In *Anthropology and Social Theory*, Sherry Ortner argues that agency is not a thing in itself, but rather, a part of a process of structuration, the continuous remaking of any cultural formation (2006: 134).[3] Structure consists of cultural resources—as well as cognitive schemas—which serve to tell individual agents what to do and how to do it in specific social contexts. Through interactions between individual agents and physical resources, the individual agents form their own schemas or sets of rules. These cognitive schemas are something to be enacted in specific contexts. Consequently, each individual agent produces new cultural resources, which can be interpreted and used by others.[4] In the case of Vocaloid fandom, Supercell's Vocaloid tracks can be cultural resources for fans; they create derivative works of Supercell's musical compositions. This "textual productivity"[5] by the fans plays crucial roles in enhancing the visibility, power, and fluidity of Supercell's "original" works. Such enhancement results in structuration of Vocaloid fandom. This dynamism of the playground comprises one of the main points of my book.

Finally, the book examines the impact of "infrastructure,"[6] including pop culture conventions and *dōjin* ("fan-circle") events on the circulation and promotion of Vocaloid products and derivative works. As Ryo said in the interview on June

21, 2011, the members of Supercell frequently appeared in annual *dōjin* events called Comic Market, and their Vocaloid works were already circulated through the *dōjin* market well before they released *Supercell*. The behavior of extremely dedicated fans (otaku, or "geek") also needs to be considered; this term originated in the 1980s from visual culture,[7] into which DTM culture is integrated (as previously mentioned, Hatsune Miku's US debut concert took place at Anime Expo, a meeting place for visual otaku). This book incorporates an analysis of the Vocaloid phenomenon into a growing body of scholarship on *dōjin*, otaku, and fan culture.[8] Offline physical spaces are indeed equally important as online virtual ones: the combination of both kinds of space enhances and empowers the creativity and productivity of individual creators working in these playgrounds. In sum, the book offers a sense of how an empowered fan base engages with interactive new media in the creative process, and how this ecosystem enhances the circulation of DTM works.

PART I

Settings

1 Hatsune Miku and DTM Culture

Much to the surprise of Crypton Future Media's founder and CEO Itō Hiroyuki (b. 1965), *Hatsune Miku* software was an instant hit, selling more than 15,000 in its first month of release in September 2007. Among the early adopters were many amateur Vocaloid producers, including Ryo, who began to use the Vocaloid technology for his own music. The results were swift: By the end of that year, Ryo had uploaded these works onto Niconico, including "Melt"; by the end of the decade, he had become a major-label artist in Japanese popular music. The Vocaloid synthesizer technology enhanced the productivity and creativity of such amateur music creators. This raises the question of *how* the synthesizer technology was invented from a cultural and historical context.

I am interested not only in showing that Yamaha's Vocaloid technology is a powerful and productive tool for its individual creators, but also in examining the processes through which the Vocaloid technology and DTM culture have been constructed. After all, it is the combination and interactions of the technology and individuals that contribute to generating and shaping today's Vocaloid culture. Human creativity contributes to the invention and development of synthesizer technology, which also becomes a nonhuman agent that helps the humans to pursue their own projects and purposes. Technology and humans thus co-produce society and culture by becoming part of structuration, the continuous remaking of social and cultural configurations (Ortner 2006: 134).[1] DTM culture has continuously been reconstructed in such processes as well.

This chapter examines the historical and cultural background behind the invention of Vocaloid Version 2, the birth of virtual pop idol Hatsune Miku, and the possible routes of Vocaloid phenomena. I contextualize the invention of the Vocaloid technology within the larger developmental processes of DTM culture since the 1980s.

Development of DTM Culture since the 1980s

From the late 1970s to the early 1980s, the futuristic sounds of digital synthesizers started to capture the attention of Japanese music lovers. The Japanese electronic music band Yellow Magic Orchestra (YMO) entered the limelight of Japanese popular music when YMO released its second album, *Solid State Survivor*, in 1979. The following year, it became the best-selling album in the country and won the Japan Record Award for Best Album. YMO's use of electronic instruments, cutting-edge effects (such as vocoders), and futuristic videos contributed to its high-tech image in Japanese society. As Michael Bourdaghs writes, their electronic compositions were "frequently used as in-store music by electronics retailers during this period [around 1980], further underscoring links between the band's image and cutting-edge technology" (2012: 187).

Electronic music bands, such as YMO, helped to popularize the use of synthesizers and digital recording technology.

By the early 1980s, these technologies were also being used among amateur music creators. In 1979, Japanese electronics company TEAC introduced the TEAC144, a four-track recorder (MTR) based on audio cassette tapes. This MTR enabled amateur music creators to overdub multiple tracks for at-home music-making. Previously, musicians would have had to use open-reel audio tape recorders to make multi-track recordings. These recorders were expensive; professional recording studios usually owned these recorders. As with elsewhere around the globe, audio cassette tapes were a representative medium of Japanese amateur music-making in the early 1980s. In addition, MIDI (Musical Instrumental Digital Interface) technology became standardized in the 1980s, enabling digital electronic musical instruments from different manufacturers to play compatibly (Müller 2015: 13). The musical data of these digital electronic instruments is recorded, edited, and played through a device called a sequencer. The development and availability of such technological devices enabled amateur musicians to create music at home.

There are some connections between Hatsune Miku and digital music-making technologies developed in the 1980s. In 1983, Yamaha introduced the DX7, the first digital synthesizer in the DX series. The DX7 employs Frequency Modulation (FM) synthesis. By the mid-1970s, John Chowning at Stanford proposed the idea of using FM in audio sound synthesis, and Stanford licensed it to Yamaha. Compared to previous analog synthesizers, Yamaha's digital FM synthesizer could produce a wide variety of tones, such as metal-striking and bell-like sounds. The DX7 included the MIDI ports, which allowed users to control it from another keyboard and via a computer music interface. Similar to the piano, the keyboard was responsive to touch—the harder a key was played, the louder the sound. In addition, the affordability of the DX7 made it easy for amateur musicians to create their own music. Crypton's Itō was one of these amateur DX7 users, having started to record his own music with it as a twenty-year-old.

Once Itō made his own demo tapes with these technological tools, he started to sell them to small record stores, which put his demos on their shelves. Record stores were among the few playgrounds for amateur musicians in the 1980s, since there was no internet at that point. As Itō explains, "I was not expecting the music to generate much revenues; rather, I was just enjoying the process of making my own works and selling them" (cited in Shiba 2014: 43). Itō's personal experience of using these technologies influenced his later career at Crypton, eventually leading to the creation of Hatsune Miku.

Furthermore, the original design of Miku uses a motif from a low-priced edition of DX7 called DX100. Miku's arm panel directly imitates that of DX100. Her aquamarine hair color is analogous to that of the indicator installed in DX7. MIDI terminals are printed on her skirt. Since Yamaha developed both the DX7/DX100 and the Vocaloid technology, these anecdotes demonstrate the close association between the Hatsune Miku phenomenon today and DTM culture of the 1980s.

The word "DTM" was used in Roland's 1988 product called "Desk Top Music System: Myūji-kun." It included a sound module, music sequencer software, and MIDI.[2] Since the 1990s, Japan has experienced growth in home recording and "indie" activities (Connell and Gibson 2003: 259). Further development of digital technologies and the availability of music-making products facilitated the activities of amateur musicians and music fans. In 1992, Yamaha released Hello! Music! (CBX-T3), and, in the same year, Kawai also released Sound Palette.

In his blog, composer, lyricist, arranger, and singer Sakuma Hirotaka (2012) wrote about his first experience of using a MIDI sound module. Sakuma bought Kawai's Sound Palette when he was a junior high school student. He used the sound module through Japanese IT company NEC's PC98 laptop. The screen size of this PC98 laptop was uncomfortably small compared to that of today's laptops. The software was designed to compose a piece consisting of a maximum of sixteen different parts; however, the limited capacity of the laptop itself did not actually allow users to compose a full sixteen-part piece. Sakuma recalled that the sound produced through Sound Palette was similar to that of the Family Computer (or Famicom), a video game console released by Nintendo in 1983. At that time, he recorded his original compositions on cassette tapes. This experience of using Kawai's Sound Palette motivated him to pursue a career as a composer; he has already produced seven music albums.

While Yamaha, Kawai, Roland, and other companies were producing sets of DTM equipment during the 1990s, the development and spread of personal computers, hard discs, and internet services also contributed to the growth of DTM culture. A blogger named "SF2K" (originally named "Sound Factory 2000") has been part of DTM culture for more than twenty years. In his blog, he writes about his personal experiences of using DTM tools since the late 1980s, and provides detailed information about these products. He acknowledges that since NEC's PC98 was prevalent among Japanese users during the 1990s, software companies produced different types of music sequencer for the PC98. He also used a

Macintosh computer with a sequencer software called *Ortina*, but Macintosh computers were more expensive than PC98 computers.

During the 1990s, the capacity and affordability of a hard disc drive experienced development. A hard disc drive dates back to the 1950s, but SF2K recalls that it became accessible to consumers in Japan, especially during the 1990s. Previously, a floppy disk was a major form of data exchange and storage, and a 3.5-inch 2HD floppy disk had 1.44MB of space. Hard disc drives in personal computers usually had between 80MB and 320MB of space.

The development of hard disc drives brought about the invention of hard disc multitrack recorders. In 1996, Roland released the hard disc multitrack recorder VS-880, including 32GB of space. Korg's D8 and Akai's DPS16 were other major hard disc multitrack recorders in the late 1990s. Released in December 1997, Akai's DPS12, for example, featured twelve-channel simultaneous playback, eight-channel simultaneous recording, and two-channel built-in multi-effector. At that time, the product cost 189,000 yen (about $1,450), but it was certainly affordable to amateur music-makers.

Also in the mid-1990s, Microsoft developed a consumer-oriented operating system (OS) called Windows 95. In November 1995, about three months after the release of its original English version outside of North America, Microsoft released a Japanese version of Windows 95. In August 1998, the company released Windows 98. Japanese users then began to use Windows OSs, replacing other OSs. Since the beginning of the 1990s, Japanese users had been making their own (*jisaku*) PCs; Windows OSs were compatible with these *jisaku* PCs, while Mac OSs were not (SF2K 2016). Furthermore, the intro-duction and spread of the internet during the 1990s marked an important shift from storing MIDI data on computers to storing and sharing them online. This development facilitated the growth of so-called "*dōjin ongaku*" (music by amateurs). We can see this *dōjin ongaku* phenomenon in a variety of video-sharing sites, such as Niconico and YouTube.

Amateur music-makers' experiences of using technological tools and products since the 1980s shaped their current musical activities. Sakuma, for instance, became a professional musician and composer, continuing to use new DTM products to make his own compositions. Over the last three decades, SF2K has also been using DTM products, and he currently runs a personal blog to share his knowledge about DTM culture in its historical context. Moreover, Itō became the founder and CEO of Crypton and created *Hatsune Miku* software.

Yamaha's Vocaloid Technology

The Vocaloid project began in March 2000. The project was originally named Daisy, paying homage to the IBM704—the first computer designed to "sing" in the early 1960s, and which sang the song, "Daisy Bell" (McCarthy 2014: 139). Kenmochi Hideki (b. 1967) led the Vocaloid project, which was a collaboration between Yamaha and Universitat Pompeu Fabra in Barcelona, Spain. Around 2000, the creation of the singing synthesizer was certainly meaningful to DTM culture. Even though music-making software at the time allowed its users to generate a variety of sounds that were very close to those of actual instruments, there was no such software that could simulate human singing voices. Also, whereas a synthesizer performer could substitute for a number of orchestral parts, amateur music-makers had to find actual singers in order to make recordings of musical pieces that employ, for example, a choir.[3]

Kenmochi's main objective was to create a synthesizer software that produced singing voices, from which lyrics could be clearly discerned. Kenmochi wanted it to produce human-sounding singing voices, not robotic ones. In 1997, Yamaha released PLG100-SG as the forerunner of Vocaloid, but this product did not solve this concern. By July 2000, the Vocaloid could speak words that contained consonants, in addition to five Japanese vowels: a, i, u, e, o. The Vocaloid then spoke the Japanese word "*asa*" (morning). Kenmochi and other project members continued to develop the technology to produce all possible mixes of phonemes of Japanese: consonant-vowel, vowel-consonant, and vowel-vowel. Yamaha also intended to make the Vocaloid technology convenient to amateur music-makers.

Yamaha did not sell Vocaloid technology directly to the public, but instead licensed it to third-party companies to use for their own technology and software. Each company could then develop and release their own Vocaloid software with their own "singer library"—a database of samples extracted from human singing voices. Since its release in 2004, several products, such as *Meiko* and *Kaito* from Crypton, and *Leon*, *Lola*, and *Miriam* from Zero-G in the United Kingdom, have been made based on Vocaloid Version 1. For Vocaloid Version 2, several products were produced and released before Crypton's *Hatsune Miku* came on sale in August 2007. These products include *Prima* from Zero-G and *Big-AL* and *Sweet Ann* from Power FX in Sweden.

Vocaloid Version 2 consists of three parts: (1) score editor; (2) singer library; and (3) system engine. Through the score editor, Vocaloid users can input lyrics, notes, and vocal expressions such as vibrato. However, it cannot simulate, for example, hoarse voices. As users type in lyrics, the score editor converts them into phonetic symbols. In Vocaloid Version 2, the users can utilize a MIDI keyboard to input musical notes, so that they "can 'play' Vocaloid with pre-defined lyrics" (Kenmochi and Ōshita 2007: 1). Vocaloid Version 2 contains a singer library, consisting mostly of an adjacent pair of phones called diaphones. These samples were extracted from human singing voices. The number of samples is approximately 2,000 for every pitch. These samples in the singer library encompass all possible mixes of phonemes of the target language. The library also includes sustained vowels. The third component of Vocaloid Version 2 is the synthesis engine, which receives score information, automatically chooses necessary samples from the singer library, and thus connects the score information and the library.

The developmental processes of the Vocaloid synthesizer entailed continuous interactions between humans and technology. In these processes, the question of what constitutes "human voices" has been continuously redefined. While humans develop technology, technological artifacts also shape human perception.

Hatsune Miku

After Yamaha announced Vocaloid Version 1 in February 2003, Zero-G released two related products, *Leon* and *Lola*, in non-Japanese markets in January 2004. In March, Crypton released *Leon* and *Lola* in Japan. Leon was a male Vocaloid, while Lola was a female Vocaloid. Both sang in English. In November 2004, Crypton released its first Vocaloid synthesizer named "Meiko," using samples of a Japanese professional singer, Haigō Meiko. On the cover of *Meiko* software is a female anime character, which Crypton had selected to appeal to Japan's large manga and anime fan bases. Within a year after release, *Meiko* had sold about 3,000 units—a relatively successful result for the digital music industry (Shiba 2014: 100). However, Crypton's next Vocaloid Version 1 product, a male Vocaloid named "Kaito" (launched in February 2006), sold only about 500 units a year. Crypton then thought that a male Vocaloid did not satisfy consumer demand, and created a female Vocaloid character—i.e., Hatsune Miku—for its next product. While Kenmochi and other project members were continuing to develop the Vocaloid technology, the project was cut back because of low demand. By 2007, only two people remained on the project, including Kenmochi.

When Yamaha announced Vocaloid Version 2 in January 2007, Crypton initiated a new project based on this updated Vocaloid technology, with its main concept: "*kakū no kyara-kutaa ga utau*" (an imaginary character sings). In contrast to Meiko and Kaito, the company decided to sample the voice of anime voice actress Fujita Saki rather than continue using professional singers. Hatsune Miku is the first Vocaloid to use an anime voice actress. Crypton's Itō said:

> I do not usually watch anime, and I am not well acquainted with otaku culture. The main reason why I decided to use an anime voice actress for this project is that I wanted to put a new value on the product and show it to the world. As a company that creates sounds, we have developed new tone colors and musical instruments. The Vocaloid is one of them. I thought that rather than a professional singer or announcer,

a voice artist would be more suitable for showing new directions of using singing synthesizer software and variations in
voice quality … By the beginning of the Hatsune Miku project,
I had already decided to use an anime voice actress.

Itō, cited in Shiba 2014: 103–4

Since they were using an anime voice actress, they developed
a new anime character. Japanese illustrator KEI designed
the virtual pop idol, giving birth to Hatsune Miku. Crypton's
intention was to make their new Vocaloid software *Hatsune
Miku* marketable to anime fan communities; with the choice
of voice and visual avatar, they also made the resulting music
suitable to this community.

What Crypton found in Fujita's voices as well as the image
of Miku was *kawaisa* (cuteness). The quality of *kawaisa* has
long been mentioned in the context of Japanese pop culture.
Its use was initially targeted for adolescent girls, or *shōjo*,
though *kawaii* (cute) characters have been omnipresent in
different cultural forms, including anime, comic books, and
video games.[4] This concept invokes kinds of "relationality," i.e.,
"ongoing connections between one person and others, as well
as with objects" (Yano 2013: 56). One kind of relationality refers
to the gazer/gazed-upon connection (ibid.: 57). The "gazer" is
a person who dubs other persons or objects, i.e., the "gazed-
upon," as being *kawaii*. In Japanese popular culture, the gazer
(i.e., a consumer) solidifies feelings of empathy and intimacy
toward the gazed-upon by obtaining consumer goods and
services associated with them. To the gazer, the persons or
objects of affection serve as a prompt for an empathetic
caregiving, and consuming these goods and services is the
way to offer the empathetic caregiving. By featuring the
character's *kawaisa*, Crypton made *Hatsune Miku* software

appealing to both individuals active in DTM culture and fans of Japanese popular culture in general.

Miku's *kawaisa* could be contextualized within the continuing development of Japanese popular idol culture since the 1960s. The Japanese popular music industry, for instance, began to feature adolescent female idols after a 1963 French movie called *Cherchez l'idole* was released in Japan under the title *Aidoru o Sagase* (Let's Look for an Idol) (Aoyagi 2005: 4–5; Galbraith and Karlin 2012: 4–5). One of the featured teen idols in the movie, Sylvie Vartan, visited Japan and became a celebrity when she released a song there. This prompted a producer in the popular music industry to create idol pop as a new popular music genre in Japan, and the music industry in Japan experienced an idol boom during the 1970s and 1980s at the height of Japan's post-war economic miracle. Since then, this musical genre has emphasized performers' adolescent personalities and cuteness. Pop idols were supposed to be life-sized (*tōshindai*); fans did not expect these female idols to become perfect stars, but rather to be the girls-next-door. Japanese pop idols sang popular songs, posed for photographs, and appeared on TV programs. Meanwhile, their other activities included handshaking (meet-and-greet) events, get-togethers with fans, and correspondence with them by letter. These activities were designed to construct and maintain "intimacy" between idols and their fans (Aoyagi 2000: 312). Fans can virtually meet Miku, whenever they use the music software with their own personal computers. In so doing, they can maintain intimacy with the virtual pop idol.

Miku is, nevertheless, distinct from those actual pop idols in the sense that users of the Vocaloid software manipulate Miku and her performance. Jennifer Milioto Matsue (2016) discerns a commonality between Miku and dolls of the *bunraku* puppet theater developed during the Edo period (also known as the Tokugawa period, 1603–1867), since both are manipulated by humans. They do not have *honne* (private self), only *tatemae* (social face). This is distinct from the case of human idols who usually receive negative media attention when they fail to hide their personal lives (Prusa 2012). For instance, Minegishi Minami, a member of Japanese pop idol group AKB48, shaved her head and posted a tearful apology video onto YouTube after Japanese paparazzi caught her dating. She broke the management's no-dating rule. Matsue writes, "Human idols must hide their personal lives from fans to maintain the illusion of their fantasy persona—they must separate the *honne* from the *tatemae*—but Hatsune Miku cannot cause trouble and draw negative media attention to her—there is no *honne*" (2016: 133, original emphasis).

Hatsune Miku software was a hit in Japan: Crypton sold more than 20,000 units within the first two months of its release, far outstripping the 3,000 units of *Meiko* it had sold in its first year. *Hatsune Miku* had top market share (more than 30 percent) in the sound-making software market by September 2007 (BCN Ranking 2007); it had sold 42,000 units by September 2008. There seem to be multiple reasons behind the success of the virtual pop star. Her cuteness certainly attracted attention from anime fans who did not have any music-making experience. Miku attracted fans not only among men but also among women. According to market research by Yamaha among Vocaloid fans in Tokyo (in Shinjuku, Shibuya, Ikebukuro, and Akihabara), 24 percent of teenage girls are frequent listeners to or fans of Vocaloid songs (AV Watch 2011). Many female fans cosplay (dress up) as Miku or other Vocaloid characters, attend pop culture conventions, and upload their pictures onto online platforms. These fans not only gaze passively at Miku but also actively imitate her cuteness and perform it in public spaces.[5] As Ian Condry puts it, we cannot fully explain this cultural phenomenon without taking into account the "social energy arising from a collective interest in Miku" (2013: 63). A year after releasing the music software, Crypton estimated that only about 10,000 to 15,000 users were active users who were actually making music with it (Famitsu.com 2008).

Meanwhile, the technical features of the singing synthesizer contributed to the growth of DTM culture. An early VocaloP, Ryo started to use Vocaloid synthesizers because as an amateur DTM maker he could not find any vocalists around him. Whereas humans control the performance of the virtual pop idol, Vocaloid technology was invented through continuous testing and interaction between humans and technology. And the Vocaloid enables its users like Ryo to enhance their musical creativity and productivity; it thus reinvigorates DTM culture, with its historical roots that date back to the rise of digital synthesizers in the 1980s.

Since the *Hatsune Miku* software became available, producers have created Miku's vocal performances through desktop computers. Where, then, are their playgrounds? Where are the spaces for these amateur Vocaloid creators and fans to display their own musical works to others? The next chapter discusses the distribution infrastructure and its impact on the creativity of Vocaloid users and the development of DTM culture. The distribution infrastructure encompasses both online video-sharing platforms, such as Niconico and Piapro, and offline pop culture conventions and *dōjin* ("fan-circle") events. They play highly important roles for the circulation of Vocaloid products and their derivative works.

2 How Creative is the "Playground"? Niconico, Piapro, and *Dōjin* Circles

Two months after the release of *Hatsune Miku*, Ryo posted his Vocaloid work on Niconico, entitled "Hatsune Miku ga 'Gravity/Sakamoto' o utatte kureta yo" (Hatsune Miku Sang Sakamoto Maaya's "Gravity" for Us, 2007). An arrangement of the song "Gravity" (2003), sung by Sakamoto Maaya and composed by Kanno Yōko with lyrics by Troy, it was Ryo's first attempt to make his own Vocaloid work available online. He wrote a short comment on Niconico:

> This is my first post on Niconico. Since so far I have rarely seen Hatsune Miku singing songs written entirely in English, I produced one. I learned the backing track by ear. I excluded the introduction and coda since I did not have enough time. I would be pleased if you could listen to this musical work.
>
> Ryo 2007

Within the short span of two months after the release of *Hatsune Miku*, VocaloPs had already begun to upload their own music and, more importantly, influence each other in this online forum, a creative and collaborative playground for amateur VocaloPs. Ryo created his own arrangement of

"Gravity" simply because he did not see any Vocaloid songs in English on the video-sharing platform. His Vocaloid work on Niconico did not include an illustration of Hatsune Miku—instead, it used the image of Sakamoto Maaya taken from the front cover of the CD. Yet by the time Ryo composed "The World Is Mine" and uploaded it onto Niconico on May 31, 2008, he had already started to collaborate with other Niconico users who were also artists and illustrators. Ryo used several illustrations of Miku drawn by one of the members of Supercell, named Redjuice, for the video clip of "The World Is Mine."

What is Niconico? How creative is it? How can we explain the creative practices of the Niconico users happening on the video-sharing platforms? I would also like to ask what enables Vocaloid users and illustrators of Miku to collaborate with each other. What, if any, are the copyright-related issues in these processes? While the last chapter has discussed the development of Vocaloid technology and *Hatsune Miku* software, this chapter focuses on the "distribution infra-structure"[1] for amateur Vocaloid producers and illustrators of Miku. The distribution infrastructure encompasses online video-sharing platforms, such as Niconico and Piapro, which are networked, participatory, and peer-to-peer. These spaces enable individual creators to circulate their works and collaborate with each other. *Niji sōsaku* (literally "secondary creation") becomes common as existing Vocaloid works have continuously been reused by other users in online communities. I also contextualize the Vocaloid phenomenon within the growth of amateur *dōjin* ("fan-circle") culture, which forms the offline side of the distribution infrastructure: pop culture conventions and *dōjin* events. The distribution infrastructure enhances the creativity and productivity of these Vocaloid creators.

It is important to remark, however, that the evolution was not cultivated by the existence and availability of the distribution infrastructure alone but nurtured through the creative practices of individual users (Tamagawa 2012: 128). Those users are individual agents who are capable of expanding their creative playground spaces by making and distributing their own online media content, attracting other users' attention, and influencing each other. Equally important is the power structure that informs individual agency. In other words, certain rules exist in those creative spaces, upon which individual agents draw. Therefore, the combination of structure and individual agency determines the potential expansion and enhancement of online playgrounds. The development of Vocaloid culture hinges not only on how individual agents use Vocaloids, but also on how they use the distribution infrastructure.

For the purpose of theorizing Niconico users' creative practices and consumption style, I incorporate Japanese cultural critic Azuma Hiroki's (2009) concept of "database consumption." In *Otaku: Japan's Database Animals*, Azuma argues that today's consumer culture, which has been maintained by interactive media, can no longer be explained with Japanese critic Ōtsuka Eiji's idea of "narrative consumption."[2] In narrative consumption, people are repeatedly consuming pieces and fragments of "grand narratives"—including, for example, episodes of anime, TV, and radio programs and a variety of anime characters and pop idol commodities—which the industries are supposed to produce and circulate. This phenomenon was particularly visible during the 1980s. Consumers aim to obtain the totality of these "narratives." This consumption model, thus, essentially places the center of knowledge production on the industry side. Azuma describes narrative consumption, as suggested by Ōtsuka, as characteristic of modernity.

Instead, Azuma proposes a database (or reading-up) model of consumption as that of postmodernity, to theorize today's consumer cultures on the internet. He argues, "Modernity was ruled by the grand narrative. In contrast, in postmodernity the grand narratives break down and the cohesion of the social whole rapidly weakens" (Azuma 2009: 28). He adds, "An easily understandable example of this [database model] is the Internet. The Net has no center. That is to say, no hidden grand narrative regulates all Web pages" (2009: 31). Consumers can spend their time reading up on subjects of interest via the internet and further aggregate fragments, pieces, and parts of relevant digital images and texts found on the database (i.e., "settings," in my terminology) into what Azuma calls "derivative works"—a term for the rereading and reproduction of the *originals* in forms of, for example, fanzines, fan games, fan figures, and so forth (2009: 25). "[D]epending on the differing modes of 'reading up' by users, consumers … can produce any number of derivative works that differ from the originals" (Azuma 2009: 33).

Azuma's view obviously overlooks the capacity of consumers of the "grand narratives" to become producers of derivative works and thus ignores any possibilities for the complexity and incoherence of Japanese consumer cultures in the pre-internet age. But what I find useful, particularly for the field of fan studies, is that the database consumption model potentially places the center of knowledge production and its circulation on each consumer—and, in my case, individual Vocaloid producers, illustrators, and fans—rather than on the industry. Although the Vocaloid technology and *Hatsune Miku* software were invented and released by Yamaha and Crypton

Future Media, respectively, musical content has been created and circulated essentially by individual users, similar to DTM culture in the 1980s. Azuma thus points out the collapse and dysfunction of the "grand narrative," i.e., the totality resting in the hands of pop culture industries. This further results in the proliferation of derivative works—copies detached from their original and the author—or what Steven Feld called "schizophonic mimesis" to refer to "a broad spectrum of interactive and extractive practices" (1996: 13). Secondary creation often blurs the line between the original and its copies.

Niconico and Secondary Creation

Niconico was originally called "Nico Nico Douga (Provisional)." It was renamed as "Nico Nico Douga (Gamma)" in March 2007 and then started to use the user ID system, offering membership to users. This update allowed its users to upload original movies on the server. Within two months or so, it reached more than one million users. By January 2009, Niconico had more than eleven million users, and more than two million video clips were uploaded onto the site (Hamasaki et al. 2010: 160).

Niwango is a subsidiary of Dwango, which was founded by Kawakami Nobuo in 1997. Their service provided polyphonic ringtones (*chaku-mero*) and vocal ringtones sampled from recordings (*chaku-uta*) in the early 2000s. The CEO of Niwango, Sugimoto Seiji, considered ringtones to be a medium for communication, rather than musical pieces one listens to alone (Shiba 2014: 120). Ringtones could become a topic for conversation, especially when one hears her/his friends' ringtones in everyday life. Similarly, Sugimoto wanted the

Niconico site to function as a space in which its users can share media content with each other and generate communication. When someone uploads a video clip onto Niconico, other users interact with each other by making comments on the video clip. Viewers must have their own accounts in order to watch video clips on Niconico, which is different from YouTube. In its user ID system, Niconico offers two types of membership: premium, which charges a fee of 540 yen (about $5) a month, and general, which is free. Premium members can upload a video of 100MB in size (*vs*. 40MB for free members) with no resolution limit and no limit in bitrate. Also, premium members receive 8GB of upload space with 1GB added each month, while free members are limited to 2GB. A majority of VocaloPs, such as Ryo, are premium members of Niconico.

Before Vocaloid works became prevalent on Niconico, MAD (Music Anime Dōga) culture flourished in this online space. MADs are the results of secondary creation, in which MAD artists extract scenes from existing anime works and combine them with popular music pieces. MAD artists are expected to acquire and show off certain video editing skills. Through those MADs, fans can see how amateur MAD artists reinterpret famous anime and musical works. However, as their works are truly derivative, there remains a copyright issue. In Japan, anime fans began to make their own MADs by the late 1970s, while in the US, the anime music video (AMV) culture developed in the early 1980s (Itō 2012: 281).

One of the most popular types of MAD among the Niconico community was derived from Bandai Namco Games' simulation and rhythm video game called *The Idolmaster*. It was originally released as an arcade game in 2005, and in January 2007 the Xbox 360 port of *The Idolmaster* became available. In the game, users create and develop their own

Japanese pop idols and arrange stage costumes. The users, however, could not have those virtual idols sing original songs. Instead, they had to use only a number of musical pieces that *The Idolmaster* features. Consequently, some of the users began to apply the technique of creating MADs to the video game. They extracted scenes from the video game in which anime idols are performing on stages and added Japanese popular songs to those scenes. Such videos are called "*aimasu* MADs" (I-master MADs). Among *aimasu* MAD producers, a user named "WakamuraP" has been a renowned figure in the *Idolmaster* fan community because of the sheer number of *aimasu* MADs he has uploaded onto Niconico and the views they have garnered. For instance, his *aimasu* MAD based on Japanese idol pop group Perfume's "Perfect Star, Perfect Style" (2006) received more than one million views on Niconico. The custom of having a username with "P" at the end has been carried on, as the Vocaloid creators are often called "VocaloPs." Shiba (2014: 123) also notes that the emergence of Niconico and the *aimasu* MAD culture prepared the ground in which the cultural practices of "producing one's own virtual pop idols" became the norm in Japanese pop culture fan communities.

Hamasaki et al. (2010) remark that Vocaloid works are distinct from MADs. While the latter are essentially remixes and mash-ups of pre-existing commercial content, including popular anime works and musical pieces, the former often encompass new content created by amateur users. Although Hamasaki et al.'s statement is true in some cases, we need to be skeptical about it. For instance, for his video clip first posted on Niconico, Ryo extracted an image of Sakamoto Maaya originally used for the front cover of "Gravity." However, in contrast to MADs, the Vocaloid phenomenon clearly shows multiple kinds of creative activity that have been integrated into the processes of producing Vocaloid works. Some compose songs for Miku (and other Vocaloid characters), some manipulate the Vocaloid technology to let Miku sing in certain ways, others draw illustrations of Miku, and some even edit Vocaloid works already available on Niconico.

Hamasaki et al. classify four types of creative activities (sōsaku katsudō): (1) songwriting (sakkyoku); (2) song creation through the Vocaloid software (chōsei); (3) illustration (sakuga); and (4) editing (henshū) (2010: 161–2). They explain these types of creative activities as follows:

1 **Songwriting**: Amateur songwriters are eager to promote their songs, but it takes time and money to produce promotion tapes with professional singers. [The] Vocaloid solves this problem. Now they can produce [recordings] with [computerized] vocalizations … [The technology] inspires amateur songwriters to publish their original songs with Hatsune Miku.

2 **Song creation**: It is not easy to make Hatsune Miku sing songs naturally. Certain techniques are necessary to tune Hatsune Miku, but it is fun [for Vocaloid users] to tune the software to create nice singing songs. They vie with each other to create them.

3 **Illustration**: The image of Hatsune Miku is a typical anime character and attracts anime fans [who often draw] their favorite characters … They produce many different scenes and facial expressions. Those with more expertise produce animation. They often use illustrations drawn by others as material for producing their anime. Some produce 2D animation and others 3D animation with 3D CG tools.

4 **Editing**: There are so many Hatsune Miku videos that some people collect them and produce summary videos, with ranking programs of Hatsune Miku videos. (Hamasaki et al. 2008: 166)

The Vocaloid technology and its distribution infrastructure have enabled amateur songwriters who cannot usually afford to produce promotion tapes with professional singers to circulate their musical works. This is a similar situation to DTM culture in the 1980s, as discussed in the previous chapter: The development and availability of digital electronic musical instruments and MIDI technology supported amateur *taku-roku* (home recording) scenes at that time—though the range of the distribution infrastructure is quite distinct. The next category, song creation, reveals that using Vocaloid technology indeed requires certain skills. Examining how each user has particular skills and techniques of manipulating the Vocaloid software allows us to make distinctions between users' media performances taking place on Niconico. Illustration is another type of creativity seen in Vocaloid works. Not only composers but also anime artists and illustrators participate in the creation of media content related to Hatsune Miku and structuration of the Niconico communities. The last category, editing, expects one to have a broader knowledge of content available on Niconico, as well as video editing skills.

Each of these four types of creative activity requires different musical, artistic, and video editing skills to be used in the processes of making Vocaloid works. An individual user, however, does not need to have all of these skills; when a user uploads her/his Vocaloid work onto Niconico, for instance, another user borrows the music and adds to it her/his original illustration of Miku, as part of secondary creation. The entire content of Niconico is not a fixed totality, but is always in a state of change. What Hamasaki et al. interpret in such creative activities is "massively collaborative creation of digital content" (2008: 165). As the collaborative hub and distribution infrastructure for productivity, Niconico allows Vocaloid producers to participate actively in the development of media content available in the online space. Henry Jenkins's (2006) idea of participatory culture might explain this phenomenon, as the rise of "interactive new media"—as opposed to "passive old media"—truly contributed to their media productivity. However, I would like to highlight that each user has different specialties. Some, for instance, specialize in illustration, while others are good at using *Hatsune Miku* software. In role-sharing, one does not have to be equipped to do every task in making a Vocaloid work.

How do the creators differentiate between Vocaloid works uploaded onto Niconico by Vocaloid artists with different specialties and interests? One could look at tags attached to each work and see what tags are commonly used and what they signify in the community. For instance, if the tag "*Miku orijinaru-kyoku*" (Miku's original song) is attached to a Vocaloid work, songs used in these Vocaloid videos are likely the creators' own compositions (Hamasaki et al. 2010: 162). Similarly, in order to differentiate their work from others, illustrators often use tags such as "*kaitemita*" ("I tried to draw [Miku]"), "*odottemita*" ("[Miku] tried dancing"), and "*Hatsune Miku 3D-ka keikaku*" ("A project of making 3D Hatsune Miku"). Those who are highly skilled in manipulating the Vocaloid technology—e.g., tuning Miku's singing voices—arrange existing popular music pieces and turn them into Vocaloid works. They make the virtual pop idol sing. Those specializing in this tuning use tags such as "*utawasetemita*" ("I tried to make

[Miku] sing"), "*kami chōkyō*" ("god-like tuning"),[3] and "*arenji kyoku*" ("an arranged piece"). Although an individual creator often plays multiple roles in the creation of Vocaloid works, these tags represent what the gist of each Vocaloid work is and thus help to make distinctions between those works.

Nevertheless, one might ask how such creators' copyrights are protected in this online community full of derivative works. As per Azuma's theory of otaku cultural production, otaku's individualized media performances are made through acts of infinite imitations and even piracy, "irrespective of their having been created by an author" (2009: 26). In fact, Crypton established some rules to deal with the issue of copyright.

Licenses

On December 3, 2007, Crypton started its Piapro website, through which users could submit their illustrations—or derivative works—of Vocaloid characters as well as their Vocaloid tracks. At that time, Crypton also published guidelines for the usage of its characters (*kyarakutaariyō no gaidorain*; Crypton Future Media 2015). Right after the release of the *Hatsune Miku* software in August 2007, Crypton received a number of inquiries asking if one were allowed to upload her/his illustration of Hatsune Miku, and what one should do if she/he discovered that others were using her/his illustration for their video clips without permission. Crypton's Itō contemplated the issue carefully because, as already discussed, to claim that these derivative works were all copyright infringements would reduce the scale of those creative activities happening on Niconico. The company decided to make rules for the purpose of advancing amateur Vocaloid producers' creative activities.

Crypton established the Piapro Character License (PCL) to allow Vocaloid creators to pursue secondary creation. This license is a contract between Crypton and each individual user. Under PCL, a user is allowed to produce her/his own illustration of Vocaloid characters that Crypton has created. In addition to Miku, these characters currently include Meiko, Kaito, Kagamine Rin, Kagamine Len, and Megurine Luka, all of which became famous following Miku's success. For example, Crypton sold more than 24,000 units of *Kagamine Rin/Len* software within nine months of its release (Famitsu.com 2008). Creators are prohibited from producing and using their derivative works for commercial purposes, from offending "public order and morals" by using these characters, and from using another person's work as if it were their own. Yet if these users agree with those rules listed on Piapro, they are allowed to download from the website illustrations and Vocaloid tracks produced and submitted by others.

A DTM composer called "jospecial," for example, posted his original tune on Piapro, with a note that reads: "Lyrics and *chōkyō-shi* wanted" (jospecial 2016). *Chōkyō-shi* refer to those who are skillful in utilizing the Vocaloid technology and thus tuning Miku's singing voice. He wanted to make a "complete" Vocaloid work by incorporating other users' lyrics and technique to tune Miku's voice. In addition to his original tune, for this posting jospecial borrowed the illustrator Syo's artwork of Miku, which was originally uploaded on July 5, 2016 and has been available for download on Piapro ever since. The Piapro site functions as a storage space for different types of creative work.

VocaloPs incorporate these illustrations, tunes, and/or lyrics into their own works and then upload them onto Niconico. For example, a VocaloP called minato uploaded "Ryūsei" (A Shooting Star) onto Niconico in January 2008. This video clip uses meloa's own illustration of Miku available on Piapro. Another Niconico user, ussy (2008), then borrowed minato's "Ryūsei" for the user's video clip. The phrase or tag "*Piapro yūkō katsuyō*" (Piapro effectively used) refers to Vocaloid songs combining with different types of artwork already available on Piapro. In these examples, we can recognize how the practice of borrowing existing user-generated content plays essential roles in the expansion of DTM culture. Also, those users who have posted their Vocaloid works on Niconico almost always explain whose illustrations and tunes they have used, provide links to these original works, and credit them for the secondary creation. In the Niconico community, VocaloPs are supposed to make contact with these illustrators and composers before uploading their derivative works onto the site. With this (implicit) rule, illustrators and composers can know how their original works have been used and incorporated into others' works—thus becoming conscious of their creative history as well as creative lineage.

In December 2012, Piapro also started to apply Creative Commons Licensing (CCL) to the illustrations of Crypton's characters, in addition to its own PCL. CCL is a "worldwide copyright project for contributing to the development of culture by expanding the range of creative works available for others to build upon legally and to share" (Crypton Future Media 2016). Crypton adapts CCL to the original illustrations of Hatsune Miku, Meiko, Kaito, Kagamine Rin, Kagamine Len, and Megurine Luka "to support open creative activities for creators all over the world" (ibid.). Hence, CCL is targeted at non-Japanese users of Vocaloid characters and differs from PCL in several ways. While users can reuse and distribute their works related to Vocaloid characters in any medium and format for non-commercial purposes, CCL expects each user to "give appropriate credit, provide a link to the license, and indicate if changes were made" (Creative Commons 2016). While PCL mostly applies to Japanese users, Crypton's application of CCL ensured that secondary creation of Vocaloid characters would not remain within Japan, but would become a global phenomenon.

Although it is important to pay attention to rules applied to certain social communities, these licenses are not actions, but guidelines for individual agents' creative activities. While this chapter so far has covered the online distribution infrastructure, the final part turns to offline social spaces for Vocaloid creators, that is, *dōjin* events.

Dōjin

In "Comic Market as Space for Self-Expression in Otaku Culture," Hiroaki Tamagawa defines *dōjin*—literally "fan-circle"—as "self-financed, self-published works created by an individual or collaboration between individuals" (2012: 108). *Dōjin* are amateur publications, self-financed for noncommercial purposes. In this sense, *dōjin* culture can be seen as a forerunner of today's Vocaloid culture in which production and circulation of Vocaloid works for commercial purposes are regulated under Piapro Character License. Comic Market has been recognized as the oldest *dōjin* market in Japan and an important distribution infrastructure that has supported the creative activities of amateur fans of anime and manga, namely otaku. Comic Market first convened in 1975, and it has been held twice a year in Tokyo, mainly for the distribution of *dōjin*. Although some participants publish professionally, they also participate in the *dōjin* events with their self-published works.

Tamagawa (2012: 127) notes that "participant" (*sankasha*) is the term upon which Comic Market heavily draws. For instance, organizers of Comic Market are referred to as staff participants, attending circles as circle participants, visiting as general participants, and even attending industry events as corporate participants. By using the term *sankasha*, all attendees share the sense that they are contributing to the construction of space for distributing their creative works (ibid.).

Comic Market forms an important part of the distribution infrastructure for Vocaloid producers today. One amateur creator group, "side_M Project," frequently participates in these events to distribute their Vocaloid works. The group's leader, IkaP (2015), announced on his website that the group would participate in Comic Market held in December 2015 and distribute their Vocaloid works in the form of CD-ROMs. They already produced their first album entitled "side_Music – Exceed Vol. I," which contains their ten original Vocaloid works. Among other Vocaloid-related works, they distribute a collection of illustrations of Vocaloid characters at Comic Market. This is also the case for Supercell. The group began to distribute a *dōjin* version of their first music album *Supercell* at Comic Market in August 2008, before it was released by Sony Music in March 2009.

As these examples show, interactive "new" media do not have a monopoly on distribution infrastructure for Vocaloid producers: older forms of media, such as CDs, books, magazines, and pictures, also help Vocaloid fans and partici-pants in *dōjin* activities gain and retain a sense of intimacy with Vocaloid works. In the introductory chapter of *Fanning the Flames*, William Kelly remarks that "fans seek intimacy with the object of their attention" (2004: 9). In this case, intimacy inheres in both the physicality and materiality of *dōjin* works available at Comic Market and in fans' virtual experiences with Vocaloid characters on Niconico. Thus, offline physical spaces are as important as online virtual ones in the development of Vocaloid culture. The combination of both kinds of space enables and enhances the creativity and productivity of individual Vocaloid producers working in these playgrounds.

Vocaloid producers who participate in Comic Market, such as Supercell and side_M Project, do not sell their music and illustrations for profit but for supporting and carrying on their activities as amateur Vocaloid creators. How is the Piapro Character License applied to the case of *dōjin* works, which are distributed at Comic Market in exchange for small monetary payments? Crypton, in fact, allows creators to sell their Vocaloid works at *dōjin* events only if it is not for profit. However, these creators need to obtain permission in the form of a "piapro link" (Crypton Future Media 2015). Therefore, Vocaloid musicians who have signed a contract with major record labels are not allowed to distribute their musical and artistic works at *dōjin* events. Crypton's purpose was to promote the growth of amateur music-making scenes by supporting secondary creation among these circles.

As we have seen, the distribution infrastructure for Vocaloid culture encompasses both online video-sharing platforms and offline spaces. Both spaces are important for Vocaloid producers' creative activities, which are highly collaborative as well as derivative. Such derivative activities are, to a certain extent, supported by Crypton's Piapro Character License system. PCL has enabled noncommercial activities of amateur creators. Nevertheless, whereas the combination of Vocaloid technology and distribution infrastructure has provided today's DTM creators with great opportunities to become highly active and visible, these are only part of the structures for individual agents. It is up to these individuals to determine how to deal with these structures, expand their playgrounds, and become prominent figures in the communities. William Sewell, Jr. (2005) argues that structure consists of both human and nonhuman resources. For a Vocaloid producer, human resources are her/his collaborators and interactors active in those creative spaces. Nonhuman resources include Vocaloid technology and software, illustrations of Vocaloid characters, users' Vocaloid works, "secondary" illustrations of those characters uploaded on Niconico and Piapro, and rules made by Crypton, among others. The following chapter focuses on members of Supercell—particularly Ryo—as individual agents.

PART 2

Supercell

3 Supercell as a Creator Group

In June 2011, the Anime News Network posted an interview with Ryo on its web forum. This short interview highlights Ryo's musical background as an amateur musician and composer as well as the process through which Ryo met the illustrators that make up Supercell. It further explains the ways in which Niconico and Vocaloid technology enhanced his musicality and supported his musical career as a Vocaloid producer. The interviewer asked Ryo about his transition from an "amateur" Vocaloid producer, who posted his Vocaloid works on Niconico just for his own satisfaction, to a "professional" one who has signed a contract with Sony Music Japan, which released Supercell's first album in 2009. The interviewer asked, "what new challenges did you face in dealing with the music industry, as opposed to the [dōjin] community?" Ryo answered as follows:

> The process took some time. From my point of view, there were a lot of administrative aspects that I never really knew about before and weren't really related to music. But they were important steps, and I had to be involved with all these aspects. However, now that I'm able to attract interviews from overseas, there are also many good points. Sony gave me the platform to take Supercell's music to a worldwide audience.
>
> Ryo 2011

This excerpt indicates that getting a contract from a major Japanese label certainly changed the direction of Ryo's musical career. The major-label association greatly increased the distribution and audience for his Vocaloid works, including overseas.

However, Ryo's success story reminds us that he has not been a part of the *dōjin* communities since he signed a contract with Sony. As discussed in the previous chapter, Crypton's Piapro Character License and the rules governing Comic Market exclude for-profit activities from their circles. Since 2009, Ryo has stopped uploading his Vocaloid works to Niconico. Yet his early works that were created in collaboration with other illustrators (e.g., "Melt," "Love Is War," "The World Is Mine," "Black Rock Shooter," and "When the First Love Ends") have remained available on the site. These works continue to hold influence on Niconico as they attract viewers to the site. For example, the music video "Melt" reached 10 million views on August 7, 2015, and its viewers celebrated this achievement. Meanings of cultural texts are continuously constructed and reconstructed through individuals' active reading and appropriation of those texts (Crawford 2004: 12). In this sense, Supercell's "Melt," "Love Is War," "The World Is Mine," "Black Rock Shooter," and "When the First Love Ends," among others, are still part of the Niconico and *dōjin* communities.

This chapter focuses on the development of Ryo's musical career, as well as the ways Vocaloid technologies and distribution infrastructure shaped this process. I apply a theory of structure and agency. As previously discussed, Sewell (2005) argues that structure consists of cultural resources, which individual agents utilize for their sociocultural practices and performances. Through continuous interaction between an individual agent and these physical resources that surround her/him, the individual develops her/his cultural knowledge, which is enacted in specific sociocultural contexts. As a result, the individual agent produces new cultural resources, which can be reread and reused by others (Yamada 2017: 34). For Ryo, resources include the members of Supercell and other collaborators active in those creative spaces, these collaborators' illustrations of Vocaloid characters uploaded and available on Niconico and Piapro, the Vocaloid technology and software, and the Piapro Character License established by Crypton, among others. My aim here is to locate these resources and understand how Ryo has utilized them in the processes of *becoming*—the ways in which individual composers, illustrators, and the cultural resources they create become known and visible to others, enhancing all socially and culturally. Online interactive platforms have increased these creators' chances to connect and collaborate in order to make, remake, refine, and circulate their own Vocaloid works.

Ryo as an Amateur VocaloP

Ryo started to compose music in his early teens, as a junior high school student in Japan. After he studied the piano for several years, his parents bought him a synthesizer for composing. When he entered high school, he started a rock band, in which he played drums. At that time, he listened to rock bands like Smashing Pumpkins and Nirvana. After he entered college in Japan, Nine Inch Nails and Red Hot Chili Peppers influenced his music. Ryo also listened to the Boom Boom Satellites (BBS), a Japanese electronic music duo, formed in 1990, consisting of Kawashima Michiyuki, a guitarist and vocalist, and Nakano Masayuki, a bassist and programmer.

R&S Records, a Belgium-based record company, released BBS's first single in Europe in 1997. Ryo particularly liked the group's strong kick drum (or bass drum) and synthetic bass sounds. Ryo also created his own arrangement of BBS's "Broken Mirror" in 2012. When Supercell released its third musical album, *Zigaexperientia*, in November 2013, a website called "Cinra. net" invited Nakano and Ryo for an interview (Shiba 2013). On this occasion, Ryo talked about his early music career and explained how he became a Vocaloid producer.

Soon after graduating from college, Ryo worked as a salesperson in an electronics company, a job that has nothing to do with music production at all. He was a *haken shain* (temporary dispatch worker) at that time. Working at a fraction of the wages of permanent employees and without the security of a contract, the temporary worker is an iconic figure that represents the precarious livelihoods of much of contemporary Japanese society.[1] Temporary dispatch workers can be viewed as a "new" or "alternative" form of social identity in Japan; they form a strong contrast with salarymen (white-collar workers, formerly with lifetime employment), who were the army behind the economic miracle of postwar Japan.[2]

While at work as a temporary dispatch worker, Ryo obtained *Hatsune Miku* software when Crypton Future Media released it in August 2007. In the interview with Cinra.net, he revealed that Vocaloid technology encouraged him to keep creating "things" (*mono*), or music.[3] After more than five years of working at the electronics company, Ryo decided to change jobs; he then found a job opening for a sound creator. To apply for the job, he had to submit ten sound effects tracks and three original musical compositions to the company. Meanwhile, he composed "Melt."

His personal experience of using various musical instruments and technologies, as well as interacting with musicians, prepared him to create "Melt." This song was Ryo's first major Vocaloid song, dating from before he formed Supercell. Uploaded on December 7, 2007, it had been viewed three million times within a year and 10 million times as of August 2015. Characterized by fast, sixteenth-note rhythmic figures, a melodious piano solo, and Miku's high-pitched singing voice, it is highly regarded among Vocaloid fan communities. These musical instruments and technologies—the piano, drums, synthesizers, and Vocaloid software—are technical objects of art with certain material configurations and functions, which are present at every stage of becoming for Ryo (cf. Simondon 1980: 12). Individual agents are always in the process of "becoming with" (Haraway 2008) such technical objects. In other words, these musical instruments and technologies were essential in allowing Ryo and his Vocaloid works to become well known and visible to others, empowering the VocaloP both socially and culturally. The story of Ryo shows that Vocaloid technology influenced the VocaloP to continue composing music. In the interview with the Anime News Network, Ryo explained the benefit of using the Vocaloid as follows:

> Vocaloid technology doesn't require one to worry about the range and the key for [singers]. It also makes it possible to [sing] songs in ranges that are often not possible for a person to sing. It may be [difficult] to understand for those who just listen, but I sense unlimited possibilities with Vocaloid technology.
>
> Ryo 2011

Here it is important to remember that Vocaloid technology itself is the result of years of experimentation between humans and (the materiality and functionality of) technologies. Individual agents continuously produce cultural resources while these resources shape the sociocultural performances and activities of these individual agents.

Formation of Supercell

The formation of Supercell was accidental. In the process of completing "Melt," Ryo was looking for some illustrations of Hatsune Miku. He used *dōjin* illustrator 119's (pronounced "hikeshi") digital work without permission in advance, as it had already been available on a content-sharing site. Ryo similarly took an image of Sakamoto Maaya for his earlier Vocaloid work, "Hatsune Miku ga 'Gravity/Sakamoto' o utatte kureta yo" (Hatsune Miku Sang Sakamoto Maaya's "Gravity" for Us). But in the case of "Melt," a Niconico user wrote a comment on the video, asking whether Ryo had received permission from 119 for this. Realizing his oversight, he then sent an apology to 119 for using his illustration of Miku for Ryo's Vocaloid work. Soon after Ryo obtained an *ex post facto* approval from 119, they started to collaborate with each other for their Vocaloid works and further invited artists and illustrators, many of whom were friends and colleagues of 119. This accident led to the formation of Supercell.

Indeed, active users of Vocaloid technology and the Niconico site often use others' works to complete their music videos of Hatsune Miku, as discussed in detail in the previous chapter. This open-ended, creative space enabled individual agents to invent new forms of artwork and gain chances to virtually encounter fellow creators and their works in the communities. Noriko Manabe uses the term "cyberspace" as "a metaphor to describe the social and informational connections made possible through the networked computers of the internet" (2015: 109). This cyberspace functions not only as a repository of music that major record companies in Japan do not normally release but also as a site for musical collaborations.[4] Individual creators along with their collaborative works enlarge and enhance the content of the Niconico site both quantitatively and qualitatively. Also, the example of "Melt" shows how important such video-sharing platforms are as a distribution infrastructure for today's DTM makers. Without the invention of such creative spaces and platforms, the Vocaloid culture could not have flourished in such productive and aggressive ways. However, even though Crypton established the Piapro Character License, the extent to which each individual creator's intellectual property is protected remains unresolved. Who owns such collaborative and derivative work? And what is the basis of any such proprietary claims?

When Ryo sent an apology to 119, the latter reciprocated by showing deep interest in Ryo's "Melt." Ryo was allowed to use 119's illustrations for his original Vocaloid compositions, which agreement was made through close communication between individual users. Thus, rules established to control practices of secondary creation, such as Piapro Character License, may serve as guidelines for those creators, but these rules do not tell us about how they actually negotiate and act with each other on the online platform.

In an interview published by online journal *Oricon Style*, Ryo said that he took the role of a composer and that others assumed the role of illustrator, and remaining members managed their website, event schedules, and publications.[5] In addition to Ryo and 119, the original members include illustrators Miwa Shirō, Huke, Redjuice, Suga, and Makū (who also makes movies), and administrative support members Heihachirō, Crow, and Glov. Later in 2008, designer Usa Yoshiki joined while 119 left the group. Ryo's Vocaloid works benefited from access to a variety of illustrators, whose artworks served as resources for Ryo. Some musical compositions on *Supercell* were inspired by existing illustrations of Hatsune Miku and other original anime characters by Supercell's members.

Ryo described Supercell with the Japanese word "*basho*" (place). Ryo considered Supercell to be a "place," rather than a "group." A group generally consists of a fixed number of people participating in certain projects. However, Supercell ideally offers *basho* in which people with similar interests can assemble—like a playground. Also, people do not always have to belong to the *basho*. Instead, they choose to participate in what is happening there if it suits them, which creates a loose collective. Therefore, even though Supercell consists of eleven creators, each music video does not always include every member of Supercell. Supercell consists of illustrators who were already active as manga artists and illustrators before the formation of Supercell. For example, Miwa Shirō has been recognized as a writer and manga artist for the manga series *Dogs* since the early 2000s, and already contributed his original illustrations to different books and magazines. In fact, each musical work on the album has been created through a collaboration between Ryo and one particular illustrator from Supercell. Ryo chooses an illustrator for a song or project. We may, therefore, interpret the roles of these artists as independent contributors to—as well as sources of inspiration for—the composer Ryo's projects, rather than as permanent members of the group.

According to the Oricon Style interview, Ryo used Miku because he had been unable to find a singer. And Ryo chose Niconico because he was a "*nikochū*" ("Niconico addict") and expected to receive many responses from the viewers. Furthermore, Miku was, at that time, the most famous Vocaloid among the Niconico communities.[6] An individual agent has intentions, and their actions are "cognitively and emotionally pointed *toward* some purpose" (Ortner 2006: 134, original emphasis).[7] Therefore, individual creators intentionally choose and utilize existing artworks and songs, as well as selecting their collaborators and content distribution platforms. These relational networks and music generated through them continuously revitalize DTM culture. They exemplify its bottom-up and open-source structures.

From *Dōjin* Market to Popular Music Industry

As discussed in the previous chapter, Comic Market serves as an important distribution infrastructure for Vocaloid producers. After Ryo uploaded "Melt" and contacted 119, both creators appeared at the seventy-third Comic Market, which was held in Tokyo from December 29 to 31, 2007. They were already calling themselves Supercell, which they likened to "a cumulo-nimbus (a towering thunderstorm cloud) whose ascending top absorbs surrounding clouds, grows rapidly, and rages for a long time" (Guitar 2007). Indeed, Supercell absorbed a number of illustrators and creators and exerted influence among Vocaloid fan communities. Yet on this occasion, only Ryo and 119 participated in the event. They sold "Melt" in CD-ROMs, along with 119's illustration of Miku.

At the next Comic Market in August 2008, Supercell circulated their first independently produced album *Supercell*, featuring a cover illustration by Miwa Shirō. This independent version of *Supercell* contained ten tracks:

1. Koi wa sensō (Love Is War)
2. Heartbreaker
3. Black Rock Shooter
4. Kurukurumaaku no sugoiyatsu (Let's Spin Wildly)
5. Line
6. The World Is Mine
7. Usotsuki no parade (A Parade of Liars)
8. Sono ichibyō slow motion (That One Second, in Slow Motion)
9. Hinekuremono (The Contrary Person)
10. Mata ne (See You Soon).

Ryo composed all music and lyrics in the music album, though he drew inspiration from existing illustrations by other members of the group. For instance, Ryo created his original song "Black Rock Shooter" based on Huke's illustration of an anime character.[8] Distinct from Miku, this anime character has long black hair and blazing blue eyes. Huke posted the illustration "Black Rock Shooter" on his blog and the online artist site Pixiv in December 2007. After he joined Supercell, he contributed his own movie based on this anime character to Ryo's Vocaloid song "Black Rock Shooter." Ryo uploaded this music video onto Niconico on June 13, 2008. Huke's character has appeared in a diversity of media content, including an original video animation (OVA), TV anime, and video game, continuously (re)producing cultural meanings.

Also, this collaboration between composer and illustrator brought about new possibilities in several ways. First, Vocaloid producers became contributors to the enhancement and expansion of otaku culture, writ large. As Comic Market was originated and developed in visual culture, composers like Ryo must work with illustrators in order to participate actively in that otaku culture. At the same time, illustrators of anime characters became active contributors to the production of online music videos, so that anime characters could appear across different media content and platforms. Vocaloid technologies, distribution infrastructure, and existing anime characters allow and inspire individual agents to create new Vocaloid works.

Since Sony released *Supercell*, Ryo's Vocaloid songs circulated much more widely among the mainstream Japanese popular music industry, or, as he put it, "*ippan ryūtsū*" (literally "general distribution"). This enhanced the visibility of VocaloPs in Japanese popular music culture, in addition to that of the pop idol, in this case, Miku.

4 Supercell's Musical Works and Visibility in Social Media

Supercell's major debut album consisted of twelve original compositions by Ryo; he added two musical works, "Melt" and "When Love Ends for the First Time," to his independently released album. In the process of producing his debut album, Ryo rerecorded all existing tracks, employing guitarist Ōkoshi Okiya and bass guitarist Tissue Hime for several songs. Sony bundled the album with a DVD that contained videos for four compositions on the CD: "Love Is War," "The World Is Mine," "Black Rock Shooter," and "Melt." It was well received in Japan: Nippon Rekōdo Kyōkai (the Record Industry Association of Japan) awarded the group a Gold Disc in June 2009, as more than 100,000 copies had been shipped within a year of release. What made the Vocaloid songs on *Supercell* distinct from other VocaloPs' works circulated on Niconico? How do we talk about the artistic quality of these Vocaloid works within the frame of fan studies?

This chapter focuses on how—and perhaps why—Supercell's Vocaloid works gained *visibility* in the Niconico community. By visibility, I mean the extent to which someone or something attracts attention on social media platforms. By studying the process of gaining visibility, we recognize the ways in which individual Vocaloid tracks are distinguished from each other. When active net users create derivative works and circulate them in social media, we recognize what Henry Jenkins calls "grassroots convergence"—"[t]he informal and sometimes unauthorized flow of media content when it becomes easy for consumers to archive, annotate, appropriate, and recirculate media content" (2006: 326). It seems that the internet has contributed to the growth of grassroots convergence. As popular-music scholar Mark Duffett writes:

> [T]he net has offered new and better ways to more easily *do what we previously did before*. What has changed is that it is hard in the Internet era *not* to see and therefore to say that fans are, at best, communicative, imaginative, communal, expert, interesting and intelligent. Online social media platforms demonstrate this in a more public and visible way than, say, talking on a mobile phone.
>
> Duffett 2014: 4, original emphasis

However, as Matt Hills (2013) has pointed out, this tendency to think that the internet makes certain fans into experts of digital content production for new media downplays questions of how these users distinguish themselves from each other on social media platforms. I use the concept of social media visibility to trace these distinctions in media content that active users perceive and discuss. Visibility of a Vocaloid work depends on the recognition its author commands in fan communities, whether or not its artistic qualities are credited to the author, and its potential for generating derivative works by other fans. Online fan discourses enhance a work's visibility. I engage in the current debate in fan studies on the textual productivity of net users.

Textual Productivity

In an essay entitled "The Cultural Economy of Fandom" (1992), media scholar John Fiske introduces a tripartite model of fan productivity: (1) semiotic, (2) enunciative, and (3) textual. Semiotic productivity alludes to the production of meaning through consuming and reading cultural texts. Enunciative productivity refers to social interactions made through both verbal and non-verbal exchanges between fans. Textual productivity encompasses cultural texts and materials created, edited, written, and developed by fans in forms such as fanzines, fan fictions, anime music videos, and so forth.[1] Fiske's populist cultural politics attempts to break the boundary between amateur and professional creators by both supporting democratizations of amateurs' textual productivity and challenging the cultural power of media professionals. Garry Crawford (2012), Cornel Sandvoss (2005, 2011), and Suzanne Scott (2008), among others, have used Fiske's pre-internet model in their studies of online fandom.

On the other hand, Matt Hills (2013) has problematized the applicability of Fiske's textual productivity to online fandom and web 2.0 production by fans. He claims: "Fiske's concept of 'textual productivity' downplays questions of fan skillfulness and competence by arguing that there is no significant, necessary difference between fans' textual productivity and official media texts with regards either to production values or skill" (2013: 133). There is also an academic debate between those who adhere to Fiske's populist cultural politics (e.g., Gauntlett 2011; Shirky 2010) and those who attempt to recuperate the amateur/professional dichotomy in opposition to Fiske (e.g., Keen 2008; Lanier 2010). One fundamental question arises from this debate: if individuals who actively engage in a variety of web 2.0 creative activities are not equally "communicative, imaginative, communal, expert, interesting and intelligent" (Duffett 2014: 4), then how do they make distinctions between their practices? In her study on amateur anime music video (AMV) culture, Itō (2012) features the presence of experienced and skilled "elite" AMV makers and their strong influence over a growing cohort of "common" or "non-elite" AMV makers. These elite AMV makers win awards at major fan/otaku conventions, through which they acquire reputation and visibility in the community (Itō 2012: 276).

Rather than looking at one's economic roles and skillfulness through the amateur/professional binary, I examine the individual agent's textual productivity, as well as the quality of actual media texts, based on how others in the community recognize and talk about these texts. The previous chapter has already shown the transition in which Ryo's "amateur" Vocaloid works turned into "professional" ones after the group released an album through Sony. Some of these works still belong to the Niconico community, where fans continue to consume and discuss them. Indeed, the amateur/professional binary is ambiguous. Whereas Fiske developed the concept of textual productivity to break the dichotomy between amateur and professional creators, I expand on this concept by drawing distinctions between individual creators and between their creative works for the purpose of recognizing their visibility in social media.

Authorship

Vocaloid fan and blogger Cobachika (2012b) posted an analysis of Vocaloid culture on his blog, writing that the emergence of "Melt" changed the way he viewed Vocaloid works.[2] Before finding Ryo's "Melt" on Niconico, Cobachika had not been conscious of VocaloPs or the authorship of Vocaloid songs. Early Vocaloid producers had used usernames such as "ika," "kz," "baker," "Oster," and so forth, but as such names did not give much of an impression of who these creators were, Cobachika could not envision them while listening to their music on Niconico. However, when Cobachika listened to "Melt," he was always conscious of its composer, Ryo. In contrast with "ika" and "kz," Ryo is a Japanese man's name, which allowed Cobachika to develop a sense of intimacy with Ryo through his music. "Melt" became visible to Cobachika, demonstrating that Vocaloid works gain visibility when they are closely connected with their creators.

Cobachika's blog post indicates not merely that certain fans prefer human-sounding usernames. More fundamentally, it shows that fans care about knowing who created particular Vocaloid songs—besides those who sing these songs in virtual space, i.e., Miku and other Vocaloid characters. Niconico requires users to have their own usernames when they create their accounts. In 2008, Niconico users started to identify Vocaloid tracks by usernames, instead of categorizing them merely as "Hatsune Miku's songs." Indeed, such VocaloPs as kz, ika, and the Oster project have become renowned in DTM culture; for example, as of August 3, 2016, ika's Vocaloid song entitled "Miku Miku ni shite ageru" (Let's All Miku Miku) (2007) received 12,333,440 views. Perhaps following suit, iTunes listed these songs with the VocaloPs' names as the artists rather than just Hatsune Miku. Vocaloid fans, including Cobachika, started to select favorite Vocaloid songs by VocaloPs' or authors' names.

The visibility on social media of VocaloPs and their works is culturally meaningful because the music and media industry in Japan tends to spotlight a group's "front person(s)" and pay little attention to others who play important roles in the processes of music production (Cobachika 2012b; see also Shiba 2014: 153–5). In contrast, Vocaloid users actively look for and remember who the lyricists, composers, and illustrators are. In general, Japanese internet users have a greater preference for anonymity than other nationalities (Manabe 2015: 115). This anonymity is prevalent on many online social media platforms. On the anonymous 2chan bulletin board, a forerunner of 4chan, users construct ironic and often nasty communication spaces, saying things they normally would not say because no one knows who they are.[3] These spaces are full of slander against public figures and minorities. Given the prevalence of anonymity on the Japanese internet, the visibility of individual users is raised by a significant margin when they are identifiable, even to such a limited degree.

However, the prevalent use of such pseudonyms as ika and kz sometimes makes it difficult for Vocaloid fans to discern the gender of VocaloPs. Anonymous net users have discussed this matter on a web forum called "Male VocaloPs and Female VocaloPs" (Hatsune Miku Channel 2016). On the forum, some users noted that DTM culture in general consisted mostly of males, and, especially in Vocaloid culture, male music-makers desired to create and manipulate their own female pop idols. This preconception seems to be analogous to what Crypton found in terms of the gender dynamics of Vocaloid culture when the company ended up selling only about 500 units of the male Vocaloid character "Kaito" within a year after its release. Crypton then thought that Vocaloid producers were mostly male, and therefore male Vocaloids did not satisfy consumer demand. Nevertheless, other users on the web forum questioned this preconception of the gender dynamics of Vocaloid culture. They mentioned the cultural impact of active female VocaloPs, including the Oster project, HitoshizukuP, and NatsuP; each of their Vocaloid songs has over one million views on YouTube. How does each user create a username/pseudonym? What meaning does she/he give to it?

As internet users tend to recognize authorship of media texts, consumers of these works tend to attribute their artistic quality to their authors. When a musical work is credited to a particular author, fans are able to talk about the characteristics of that work as belonging to a type attributed to a specific author. Such discussion would not have happened if anonymity had remained prevalent in the Vocaloid community, as in 2chan.

Artistic Quality

The original version of "Melt," which Ryo uploaded onto Niconico in December 2007, has been widely discussed on web forums, particularly its lyrics. On the online "Vocaloid Wiki," anonymous Vocaloid fans have written a synopsis of the lyrics of "Melt" in English:

> "Melt" is about a shy girl who is in love with a boy. In her pursuit of him, she gets her bangs cut and hopes he will notice, all the while encouraging herself to look cute. Her love is pure … Then, it rains. She has a collapsible umbrella in her bag, which she thought was too small, but the boy joins her under the umbrella of his own will. Heart pounding, she is so happy she could cry, because in Japan sharing an umbrella is a sign of shared feelings and associated with couples. When they reach

the station, she almost tells him to hold her because she does not want to leave him …

Wikia 2016

The lyrics of "Melt" made some Vocaloid fans, such as Cobachika, wonder what Ryo was alluding to in his song. In particular, many fans became curious about the relationship between the main character (the shy girl) and Miku. Did the girl represent the virtual pop idol Miku herself? Had Ryo intended to let Miku sing a song about herself? Or, since he never uses any keywords in the lyrics that refer specifically to Miku, was Ryo depicting a different figure? Was Ryo employing Miku to express the feelings of the shy girl through Miku's voice? In his blog, Cobachika denies any connection between the girl in the lyrics and Miku. He writes, "Miku sings only about the girl and does not mention herself. 'Melt' is not a song about Miku" (2012c).

Cobachika regards Miku not only as an actual human pop singer rather than a virtual one, but also as a being acting of her own will in virtual space. In other words, Cobachika interprets Miku as a conscious and purposive subject in her performance of "Melt," even if this virtual pop idol was invented by Crypton and manipulated by the VocaloP Ryo. I call such a construction in Vocaloid music culture *virtual subjectivity*, in which individuals imagine (or are compelled to imagine) that virtual characters are able to perform based on their own free will in virtual space. This concept is centered on perspectives in which individuals conceive of agency in a software-generated product and relevant cultural phenomena. In this sense, fans are seeing the virtual character—rather than the Vocaloid producer—as the interpreter of the lyrics, even though the latter is programming the nuances of the Vocaloid's performance.

Ryo's Vocaloid videos on Niconico often include the following phrase: "*Hatsune Miku ga orijinaru kyoku o utatte kureta yo*" (Hatsune Miku sang an original song for us). Ryo used this phrase in the videos for "Melt," "The World Is Mine," and "Black Rock Shooter." This tendency has partly contributed to the construction of virtual subjectivity among the fan community; other VocaloPs later uploaded their own Hatsune Miku songs onto the video-sharing sites and included the phrase on their titles. Fans' online discourses then emphasize Miku's subjectivity and actuality. Rafal Zaborowski's recent study on Hatsune Miku fandom shows that Miku is a fan creation both "musicwise (as songs can be created by anyone) and personalitywise (as fans dynamically shape the Miku persona)" (2016: 120). Zaborowski's ethnographic data also reveal that fans try to understand the feelings that the virtual idol expresses by listening closely to her singing; a Vocaloid fan said to Zaborowski that Miku sometimes sounded sad, and sometimes sounded angry (Zaborowski 2016: 123).

Another example is "Black Rock Shooter." Inspired by Huke's original illustration of the anime character "Black Rock Shooter," Ryo intended to depict a sixteen-year-old girl who is standing alone in the dark, afraid to move forward. She struggles to find light in darkness—and to imagine the future. In the lyrics, she continuously calls "Black Rock Shooter," from whom she takes courage to move forward. Ryo wrote that the main character of "Black Rock Shooter" is not a reference to Miku, despite the fact that Crypton originally introduced Miku as a sixteen-year-old girl. Instead, Ryo claims he was attempting to represent his own feelings toward his professional life as a VocaloP in the lyrics. He sometimes finds himself with the desire to escape from reality and cease his music-making. At the same time, he acknowledges that music-making is indeed an important means to express himself in ways he could never have done before, and thus it is a means to move forward. The interpretation of "Black Rock Shooter" is available on an online information-aggregation site called *Nico Nico Pedia* (2012). Registered users visit this website to gather fragments of information about Vocaloid lyrics and to add their own comments—thereby collectively constructing knowledge about particular Vocaloid pieces.

Ryo's lyrics are distinct from other VocaloPs' works. Take the song "Koisuru Voc@loid" (A Vocaloid in Love) by the Oster project (also known by her Niconico username, Fuwafuwa Cinnamon). Its music video was another early Hatsune Miku offering, uploaded onto Niconico in September 2007, only a few weeks after *Hatsune Miku* software was released. Its lyrics depict the "intimate" relationship between the Vocaloid Miku and an individual *Hatsune Miku* software user. The "I" in the lyrics refers to Miku herself, and "you" refers to the user. In the lyrics, Miku explains that, under the control of the user, she sings any song composed and inputted. She wants to continue this relationship because she loves the user. In contrast, fans think the "I" in "Melt" does not refer to Miku; instead, "Melt" evokes a third person, one whom Miku is depicting. This approach can open up possibilities both for Vocaloid producers, who generate a variety of song styles, and for Miku, who then acts out various roles, showing Vocaloid fans her capacity to interpret and embody these roles through her singing. By virtual subjectivity, I refer not just to the virtual pop idol performing like an actual pop idol, but rather the capacity of the Vocaloid to engage in a wide range of performative acts. Such beliefs and perspectives are constructed through fans' active readings and interpretations of Vocaloid works. Through online discourses, Vocaloid fans like Cobachika highlight specific content and increase its visibility.

Lyrics constitute a crucial part of online fan discourses on the artistry of Vocaloid works, but fans also discuss the musical characteristics of these works, which similarly increase their visibility in the Vocaloid community. As Cobachika already knew of Ryo's background as a drummer, he focused on the drum parts and rhythmic figures in his discussion of Ryo's pieces. He found the rhythmic figures of the Niconico version of "Melt" to be complicated:

> This tune ["Melt"] employs intricate drum patterns. I felt that a simple eight-beat rhythmic pattern would suit this kind of music. Although it starts off simple, it gradually gets complicated as the voice enters. Since the drums have such complicated rhythms, some listeners might hear that the drums are interfering with the singing voice.
>
> Cobachika 2012a

Cobachika seemed attracted to the intricacy of the drum part. Comparing the Niconico version of "Melt" with that released by Sony, Cobachika was disappointed (*genmetsu*) by the latter. For Cobachika, its drum part was too simplified—in his words, "tidied up" (*seiri sareta*)—which lacked excitement. Listening closely to the piano on the Niconico version of "Melt," he found that the lower-pitched notes on the piano were emphasized more than those on the bass guitar; he particularly liked its interlude section in this regard. Because of this emphasis of the piano, Cobachika described this track as "keyboard rock" (*kenban rokku*).

Steven Feld's concept of "acoustemology" conjoins acoustics and epistemology to explain the practice of "listening as a knowing-in-action: a knowing-with and knowing-through the audible" (Feld 2015: 12). As "relational ontology," acoustemology takes sound as situational, located in a specific and often intricate network of relations among subjects and/or objects (Feld 2015: 13). Such knowing takes place in a space that is co-produced among Ryo's musical work, audio technology, sound, and Cobachika's perception. Further, the knowing becomes even more powerful when it leads individuals into the act of creation. Acoustemology is about the process of knowing through sound. This knowledge, obtained through such an act of knowing, then enhances the textual productivity of fans. Listening can be part of the process that creates ideas, texts, spaces, connections, and communities. Listening is not only about knowing itself, but also about the prospect of creation.

Japanese "light novelist"[4] Sunagi Izumo is also one of those Supercell fans who actively listen to the group's Vocaloid works and write critiques of them. On March 4, 2009, the same day that Sony released *Supercell*, Sunagi wrote an essay about Ryo's Vocaloid works on his blog. Like Cobachika, Sunagi recognized that Ryo has written a number of lyrics that commonly depict "*koisuru onnanoko*" (girls in love) to let Miku represent those girls' feelings, as he does in "Melt," "The World Is Mine," and "When the First Love Ends." He acknowledged that Ryo's skill in manipulating the Vocaloid technology (i.e., tuning Hatsune Miku's singing voices, or *chōkyō*) was not perfect. Yet, according to Sunagi, this "imperfection" enabled Miku to properly represent feelings of "adolescent girls in love" in virtual space.

Sunagi pointed out that Ryo's Vocaloid songs are, in general, difficult for amateurs to sing because they cover wide ranges in pitch and do not have enough rests for breathing. The melodic range of "Love Is War," for example, stretches from A3 (just below middle C) to D5, producing an interval of an octave and a fourth between these notes. Moreover, that of "Melt" stretches from A3 to A5, an interval of two octaves. Fans are interested in knowing the melodic ranges of Vocaloid songs; there is a website called "On'iki deeta matome site" (An Aggregation Site for Melodic Range Data) on which anonymous users have created a list of Vocaloid songs along with their melodic ranges. As of August 13, 2016, the list has a total of thirty-two Hatsune Miku songs composed by sixteen different VocaloPs, including kz, the Oster project, and Ryo.[5] This site is designed for those who want to determine whether they are capable, in terms of melodic ranges, of singing certain Vocaloid songs. This list includes "Melt" (with its melodic range stretching from A3 to A5), "The World Is Mine" (from A#3 to D#5), "Black Rock Shooter" (from G#3 to D#5), "Love Is War" (from A3 to D5), and "When the First Love Ends" (from A#3 to D#5). By looking at the list, we can determine Ryo's preferred melodic ranges for Vocaloid songs.

Sunagi's critique and the information-aggregation site suggest—at least at the time Ryo created *Supercell*—not only that his songs were not suitable for amateurs to sing, but also that fans have attempted to sing songs that were originally designed for Vocaloids to perform in virtual space. Indeed, since the winter of 2007, karaoke company Xing's Joysound system first included two Vocaloid songs: Oster project's "Koisuru Voc@loid" and ika's "Miku Miku ni shite ageru." Ryo's songs became available in karaoke form as well. In Joysound's annual karaoke rankings, his "Melt" was ranked ninth in 2009 and seventh in 2010, and "The World Is Mine" was ranked tenth in 2010.[6] While only "Melt" reached the top ten of the 2009 chart among other Vocaloid songs, the 2010 chart included Vocaloid songs composed by other VocaloPs. These songs include "Magnet" composed by minato and sung by Megurine Luka and Hatsune Miku; "Ura-omote lovers" (Two-Faced Lovers) composed by wowaka and sung by Miku; and "Roshin yūkai" (Nuclear Meltdown) composed by iroha and sung by Kagamine Rin. This cultural phenomenon shows that in addition to Miku, other Vocaloid characters have gradually gained recognition among fans since 2009. Also, the karaoke technology led to the construction of spaces in which Vocaloid fans' performative acts take place.

Fans recognize and interpret the artistic quality and notable features of VocaloPs' works in their own ways. These interpretations and textual products that constitute a part of fan online discourses, highlight the visibility of Vocaloid works on online platforms. Such acts of knowing and interpreting Vocaloid works do not take place just on the individual level. A recent Vocaloid phenomenon shows that the interactive nature of Niconico enables its viewers to watch, listen to, and evaluate Vocaloid works collectively, so that they together participate in consuming them. As previously mentioned, Niconico allows viewers to leave comments at specific points of the videos, so that subsequent viewers can see them scroll across the screen. What viewers on the Niconico site usually call "*danmaku*" (literally "barrage") is internet slang that refers to a specific point in a music video, where many viewers leave the same words on the screen at the same point—which, to some viewers, might look like "bullet curtains." A good example of fan *danmaku* is Ryo's "The World Is Mine." "The World Is Mine" is a song about a girl who believes that she is the most powerful princess in the world and that the world revolves around her. The song depicts her internal struggles as she falls in love with a boy. In the music video, Miku appears to be interpreting and expressing the complex feeling of this spoiled princess. The video has several examples of *danmaku*, the most recognizable and largest of which occurs at the end, where Miku sings "ah" on a long high note. Between 4:00 and 4:07 on the video, the screen is filled with the vowel letter "a." A similar *danmaku* filled with the letter "a" occurs between 1:41 and 1:45, where Miku also sings "ah" on a long high note before the second verse begins. In addition, some words from the lyrics frequently appear in the form of *danmaku*, like "*sekaide*" ("in the world") at the beginning of each chorus (e.g., 2:22–2:26; 3:25–3:29). Other *danmaku* words include "*purin*" (Japanese pudding), "*kawaii*," "*anone*" ("you know what"), and "*chotto*" ("hey"); some of these represent the cuteness of the main character and a gendered performative act (Butler 1990).

The significance of *danmaku* on Niconico is that viewers do not just listen to a musical work individually but also evaluate it collectively. More specifically, they collectively determine the most crucial, exciting, attractive, or climactic points of the track. Subsequent viewers of the video see the *danmaku*, prompting them to also recognize the highlighted spots, visually and perhaps sonically. This sociocultural phenomenon has become prevalent in Niconico, thanks to the text scrolling feature developed by Niwango. However, the ways that users apply this text scrolling system can be diverse, depending on specific channels and even specific videos. For instance, in the music video for "Black Rock Shooter," fans create *danmaku* made up of countless star emoji. This example of *danmaku* represents the lyrics in which the sixteen-year-old girl finds stars and promises to move forward in the darkness. The title of the music video on Niconico has a star emoji. This kind of textual production may shape the way viewers see and hear Vocaloid works, while, at the same time, it enhances their visibility and plays crucial roles in differentiating Vocaloid works.

Derivative Works and Spreadability

In *Spreadable Media: Creating Value and Meaning in a Networked Culture*, Henry Jenkins, Sam Ford, and Joshua Green develop the concept of "spreadability" to understand internet users' capacity and tendency to share social media content "for their own purposes, sometimes with the permission of rights holders, sometimes against their wishes" (2013: 3). The idea of spreadability recognizes the agency of media users who can also create, remake, and spread existing media content across different media platforms. This idea contrasts with that of "stickiness," which describes online business models that keep one's attention in a certain online location in order to make advertising revenue or sales, and "mechanisms motivating people to seek out and spend time at a particular site" (Jenkins, Ford, and Green 2013: 4). The concept of spreadability emphasizes the participatory behavior of individuals on social media and the ways they enhance the visibility of ever-circulating media content. Social media platforms are resources that play crucial roles in this spreading process.

The concept of derivative works can help us examine how fans reproduce Vocaloid works and circulate them among different social media platforms. As previously discussed, a derivative work refers to a rereading and reproduction of the original in forms such as fanzines, fan games, and fan figures. Ryo's Vocaloid works are spread in part by active fans who create a plethora of derivative works and share them on online platforms.

In one such phenomenon, fans sing along with pre-existing Vocaloid recordings, then record and upload their karaoke versions on Niconico and YouTube. Fans often label these karaoke videos as "*utattemita*" ("I tried to sing it"). For instance, in January 2015, the Niconico user "JP" uploaded his karaoke version of Ryo's "Melt," which he titled "Utattemita: 'Melt' (Male Ver.)." In the video, JP sang "Melt" an octave lower in the original key of F major. He also provided a link to Ryo's original video, calling him the "*honke*" ("original maker"). JP uploaded the same music video on YouTube. As of August 16, 2016, the music video on Niconico received 350 views, and the video on YouTube received 5,200 views. The video on YouTube received more views than the one on Niconico because, unlike YouTube, Niconico only allows its registered users to access it. Another example of *utattemita* is an arrangement of "Melt" sung by eight male users: neko, piko, nodoame, halyosy, doM, jakku, ten, and pokota (youhey 2009). Often called "Niconico chorus," this music video was originally uploaded onto Niconico in May 2009, and as of August 17, 2016, it had received 429,500 views. These users borrowed an existing karaoke arrangement, "Band Edition," and Hatsune Miku illustrations by NOA (2008). Other users have reproduced this music video on YouTube. None have claimed rights to it, instead providing a link to the original maker(s).

So many derivative works of Supercell's "Melt" are available on these video-sharing sites; searching "Melt utattemita" on YouTube yields approximately 68,200 results as of August 2016. Most of them have already received more than ten thousand views. One of these *utattemita* videos received more than four million views on YouTube.[7] This cultural phenomenon demonstrates that Vocaloid videos are spreadable across different video-sharing sites, continuously constructing their derivative works and, thus, enhancing their visibility in online space. It also reveals how these interactive media and distribution platforms provide net users with opportunities to *perform* in front of a particular set of observers or audiences (Goffman 1959). The next chapter, in this regard, discusses performative aspects of Vocaloid fandom by further looking at spreadable derivative works.

PART 3

Performance

5 Hatsune Miku Fans' Performative Acts

Becoming a fan is a process of immersion into cultural texts. Fans collect objects of affection in the form of consumer goods, services, and personal memorabilia while accumulating knowledge about them. Gaining such knowledge in the process of collecting is essential for fans to cultivate feelings of intimacy toward the objects of affection (Yano 2002, 2004). This drive toward intimacy pushes individual fans to behave in certain ways and play parts "in ways that go beyond the bounds of self to seek greater communion with the object of their adoration" (Yano 2004: 44). At these moments, they might also be seeking ways of exposing their knowledge about the objects and expressing their identity as fans, which is something to be enacted and performed "on the surface of the body" (Butler 1990: 136).

This chapter explores the ways in which fans of Vocaloid characters like Hatsune Miku construct their own identities through creation and performance. The performative aspects of Vocaloid fandom is not only a "thing" to be picked over analytically, but also an identity construction which is perpetually claimed and disclaimed and which performs cultural work (Hills 2002: xi). Drawing on Judith Butler's performative theory of identity construction, I believe that fans perform their identity, and that the effects of this identity are produced through repeating acts, which serve as processes of self-construction and self-formation. While concert venues are spaces for pop idol performances, they are also spaces where each fan constructs her/his identity and plays her/his part. The fans, too, are on a stage: they perform before observers and fellow fans, which motivates their participation and knowledge sharing.

Miku and other Vocaloids perform not only in virtual space but also in concert halls. On August 31, 2009, two years after the release of *Hatsune Miku* software, the talent agency[1] INCS toenter, which manages the members of Supercell, organized MikuFes '09 (Summer), a Vocaloid music event which also featured other DTM/Vocaloid creators, including Livetune (led by kz), the Oster project, and Deadball-P. At the event, Miku was projected onto a screen in front of more than 2,300 fans with green light sticks in their hands at Studio Coast. On this occasion, Miku and her live backing band (electric guitar, bass, drums, and other instrumentalists) performed several pieces from *Supercell*, including "The World Is Mine," "Melt," "Love Is War," "Black Rock Shooter," and "When the First Love Ends." Concert halls became new playground spaces for those associated with the development and expansion of Vocaloid culture, including VocaloPs, illustrators, and other collaborators. Vocaloid fans also performed their parts in these spaces.

Hence, the Vocaloid is not alone in the performance at the concert, but is joined in performance by active fans, whose expressive practices happen to be a less spotlighted part of pop idol performance. Scrutinizing fans' behavior and activities provides another lens through which to consider the performative aspects of popular music fandom. Erving Goffman (1959) refers to "front regions," or occasions where social interactions and performances take place under public scrutiny, and each individual becomes an actor in front of a particular set of observers or audiences. In front regions, fans watch and care about other fans' behavior and performance. In Vocaloid music culture, front regions include both the offline social spaces of the concert and the online spaces of Niconico, YouTube, online forums, and personal blogs, among others, which exhibit the wide range of fans' performative spaces in the age of continuously circulating new media.

Front Regions and Performance as a Way of Knowing

In *Idol Performance and Symbolic Production in Contemporary Japan*, symbolic anthropologist Hiroshi Aoyagi describes *aidoru otaku* ("idol geeks")—a "conspicuous group of idol worshippers" (2005: 205). He explores their main activities as consumers of J-pop idol culture, such as extensive collection of pop idol goods, habitual attendance at pop idol concerts and fan conventions, and participation in voluntary support groups and events organized by "idol study groups." Some idol fans publish their own magazines and newsletters "as ways of exposing their knowledge about, and their dedication to, their idols" (Aoyagi 2005: 205). These are the essential activities of idol fans.

In addition, Aoyagi shares with readers his observation of enthusiastic fans reacting during a live performance of a J-pop idol (2005: 226). Although he does not explain these fans' performance meticulously, his ethnographic account provides some hints of what we could further examine—e.g., costume and items to be used during the performance—in order to understand "identification as an enacted fantasy" (Butler 1990: 136).

Erving Goffman considers "personal front" and "appearance" as fundamental parts of an individual's performance in front regions. In *The Presentation of Self in Everyday Life* (1959), Goffman defines "personal front" as "items of expressive equipment, the items that we most intimately identify with the performer [herself/himself] and that we naturally expect will follow the performer wherever [she/he] goes. As part of personal front we may include: insignia of office or rank; clothing; sex, age, and racial characteristics; size and looks; posture; speech patterns; facial expressions; bodily gestures; and the like" (1959: 24). Goffman's concept of personal front could encompass such performative acts of Vocaloid fans as which costumes they wear to concerts, what items they bring, and how they wave during the show. Such "appearances" are "stimuli which function at the time to tell us of the performer's social statuses" (Goffman 1959: 24); in other words, appearances reveal the *performer*'s state and convince others of one's identity as a fan.

Cosplay has become a worldwide phenomenon. Anime otaku dress up as their favorite anime characters, participate in pop culture conventions and *dōjin* events, and get their pictures taken. These anime conventions are "the ultimate events for anime otaku," according to Lawrence Eng (2012: 173).[2] In this front region, fans perform in front of other anime otaku and influence them. Conventions and concert venues are stages for otaku to play roles, including dressing up in costumes.

As discussed in Chapter 1, Crypton used Miku and other anime characters with the intention of making their Vocaloid software marketable to anime fan communities. Consequently, Vocaloid works are sold at Comic Markets and *dōjin* events, while Miku and other Vocaloid characters perform "live" at anime conventions. On such occasions, some fans of Vocaloid characters create their own costumes by imitating those worn by Vocaloid characters. Vocaloid fans attend J-pop culture events with these costumes, socialize, and take photos with others. A Hatsune Miku costume by fans may include a long aquamarine wig, a collar vest with a tie in aquamarine, a black pleated skirt, black knee high socks, and headphones. These costumes and accessories are derivative works, as they reread and reproduce the original Hatsune Miku. They all function as personal front and appearance, which communicates the wearer's identity as a Hatsune Miku fan. Such derivative works are thus integral parts of a fan's performance. Furthermore, J-pop idol fans often carry "Cyalume" light sticks in concerts and wave them in specific ways, in a performative act sometimes called "*ota-gei*" ("otaku's performance"). Hatsune Miku fans bring to concerts light sticks in the idol's color of aquamarine.

There are also local events where VocaloPs, DJs, illustrators, and fans display their Vocaloid-related works and perform their identities. For example, since March 2015, Vocaloid Fan Club has organized a series of Vocaloid events in a live entertainment space called nagomix in Shibuya, Tokyo. These events are aimed at producing spaces in which Vocaloid fans gain opportunities to meet and interact with each other and to vitalize the local fan community. On these occasions, DJs and VocaloPs play their remixes of existing Vocaloid pieces, and fans wear and show off their own Hatsune Miku costumes and perform *ota-gei*.[3]

The performative practices of one day affect and shape Hatsune Miku fans' practices of the next. On March 15, 2010, six days after attending "*Miku no hi kansha-sai*" (Miku's Thanksgiving Festival) at Zepp Tokyo, the Niconico user lollipop posted an instructional video on making a DIY light stick.[4] At the concert venue, she had seen other fans waving Y-shaped light sticks that looked like leeks ("*negi-lume*"), which inspired her to make her own. Hatsune Miku fans recognize leeks as one of her "character items"—an item that ties to specific images of an anime or manga character.[5] In the Niconico video clip, lollipop listed all items used to make the negi-lume, including clear plastic tubes, green transparent sheets used to cover the inside of the stick, and batteries, and explained how she utilized them. As an "observer," lollipop learned of other fans' performative acts and contributed such an instructional video to others participating in Hatsune Miku fandom.

For Goffman, performance encompasses "all the activity of an individual which occurs during a period marked by [her/his] continuous presence before a particular set of observers and which has some influence on the observers" (1959: 22). Fans perform under public scrutiny in a manner "proper" for their observers (i.e., other fans), who, in turn, also become "performers" in the community. They are thus motivated to shape their future behavior and performance in front regions. Knowledge about fan practices comes from doing or performing *with* others. In this sense, performance can be a way of knowing.[6]

Cultures of Circulation and Construction of Front Regions on the Net

The case of lollipop further raises questions regarding circulation in the context of performance studies. How do we think about the circulation of knowledge, ideas, and media content as part of sociocultural performance? How does circulation contribute to the construction of front regions? Where are these spaces located? In *Japanoise: Music at the Edge of Circulation* (2013), David Novak utilizes the concept of circulation not only to describe the flow of material goods but also to capture the broader dissemination of knowledge, ideas, and cultural content. In the process of circulation, cultural content is continuously produced. Therefore, circulation is "performance," not just "movement" or "exchange" (Novak 2013: 17). As "a nexus of cultural production" (Novak 2013: 18), circulation itself forms culture "at the edge," and in this sense, it generates new spaces for performative acts. As Novak asserts, the edge represents "transformational places where new possibilities open up again" (2013: 19). This "edge" of circulation is where "cultural feedback" occurs. This "feedback" can be creative practices and performances of musicians and audiences, and thus sustains the circulation of musical works in multiple forms and ways.

Benjamin Lee and Edward LiPuma coined the term "cultures of circulation" to further expand the meaning of circulation from its conventional use as a "movement of people, ideas, and commodities from one culture to another" (2002: 192). For them, circulation is a cultural phenomenon—a "cultural process with its own forms of abstraction, evaluation, and constraint, which are created by the interactions between specific types of circulating forms and the interpretive communities built around them" (2002: 192). The concept of cultures of circulation helps us see the performativity of circulation; circulation generates a cultural phenomenon and performance, which connect to the construction of meanings and transmit them. Thus, based on the perspectives of Novak (2013) and Lee and LiPuma (2002), circulation can connote both the emergence of cultural performances and products, and their movements.

Ryo's "Melt" has continuously been circulating among fan communities through both "passive old media" (e.g., CDs) and "interactive new media" (e.g., Niconico). This circulation results in cultural feedback in the form of media texts, including fan-made movies and video clips based on the song. Fans not only obtain "Melt" but also create new media content by "making do" with it.[7] In the process of circulation, both original and derivative works turn into cultural resources, which are read and adapted by their audiences. At these edges of media circulation, individuals construct their own creative, inter-active, and performative spaces, where fans perform in front of observers and audiences and front regions are formed.

Are Goffman's ideas of front regions applicable to the analysis of Vocaloid fans' online activities? One might want to interpret them as part of the "back region" (Goffman 1959), which is considered, in essence, not to be under public scrutiny, because such activities in virtual spaces seem more "private" compared to actual spaces. Nevertheless, fans' online activities and interactions can also be interpreted as perfor-mance occurring within the frame of front regions. Online video-sharing platforms are front regions for Vocaloid fans, so long as derivative works (e.g., of "Melt") are uploaded onto them *and* become available and accessible to audiences who provide critiques of these performances. The *utattemita* ("I tried to sing it") phenomenon illustrates this idea; the Niconico user JP's (2015) karaoke version of Ryo's "Melt" is not only part of JP's textual production but also JP's sociocultural performance in front of his audiences.

In addition to *utattemita*, there is another kind of "cover" video clip called "*hiitemita*" ("I tried to play it"). In *hiitemita*, internet users play their own arrangements of musical pieces with their own instruments, such as piano, guitar, and bass guitar. These performers receive comments from their audiences. In April 2009, Marasy uploaded his performance of "Melt" on piano onto YouTube. Having started uploading his performances on

Niconico and YouTube in 2008, he was already recognized as a "Niconico pianist," a tag often attached to this kind of video clip. Along with his numerous uploads, he has also released his music on CD albums like *Marasy Piano World* (2014) and *Logistic Function: Vocaloid Songs Compilation* (2015), both of which contain piano covers of Vocaloid pieces by well-known VocaloPs. In "'Melt' hiitemita" ("I tried to play 'Melt'"), Marasy plays his own solo arrangement, while putting on his piano a stuffed pink monkey and a leek as Miku's character item. As of June 2, 2016, the video clip on YouTube received 1,944,100 views, 8,861 thumbs-ups, 107 thumbs-downs, and 907 comments indicating a positive reception. Many comments include "*kami*" (literally "god"), which internet users invoke to note outstanding performance or creative skills (see also Chapter 2).

Marasy's piano performances of Vocaloid songs circulate among English speakers through the internet. The blogger Senderista founded the website "Marasy8 Fans," which aggregates every *hiitemita* movie of Marasy online as well as transcriptions in staff notation by other users. As Senderista wrote in English on the website:

> Here, I will publish all the sheets of Marasy8 I find! You just click the link and you have the file :) To find better the songs you want, go through the gadget "blog archive" ;).
>
> Senderista 2016

Such an attempt to create additional spaces in the form of personal blogs contributes to the (re)construction of new front regions for Marasy as a performer. In addition, the continuous circulation of Vocaloid works generates new cultural resources which are to be read and used by their audiences, thereby opening up new spaces for Vocaloid fans' performative acts.

Transnational Circulation of "The World Is Mine" and Friction

Marasy's case suggests not only the possibility of broad circulation of Supercell's works but also the emergence of cultural feedback in the form of musical performance in transnational contexts. Indeed, Supercell's Vocaloid works have been adapted by singers across the world.

In November 2015, Rebecca "Becca" Emily Hollcraft—a US-based singer-songwriter—posted her own English cover of Supercell's "The World Is Mine" onto YouTube.[8] For the performance, Becca cosplayed by dyeing her hair aquamarine, like Miku. Miku and Becca had previously collaborated on "Shibuya," a song composed by Becca and released in August 2009, almost a year after Becca released her first full-length album *Alive!!* (2008) from Sony Music Japan. Since Supercell's "The World Is Mine" was one of her favorite songs, and she had connections with Japan, she decided to create her own version of the song in English with a few words in Japanese.

As of June 5, 2016, the video clip had 147,860 views with 4,312 thumbs-ups, but it received criticism as cultural misappropriation. The user Mekiko Senpai wrote:

> It doesn't matter the race[.] [Becca] should pronounce the words correctly. It's [a] matter of respect … It's annoying and disrespectful when people mispronounce words, especially now when you could easily search how to say them.
>
> Becca Official 2015

Mekiko Senpai criticized Becca for her inability to pronounce Japanese words correctly. Instead of singing the entire song in English, Becca kept some Japanese words like "*yone*" (right?), "*sono-ichi*" (the first), "*sono-ni*" (the second), and "*sono-san*" (the third) from Ryo's "The World Is Mine." This mix of Japanese and English is not unusual in J-pop. These Japanese words were highlighted with *danmaku* (see Chapter 4) on Ryo's video clip of "The World Is Mine" (2008) on Niconico. Moreover, Becca inserted the Japanese phrase, "Hatsune Miku *kawaiitte*" (that Hatsune Miku is cute), at the end of the first verse. Her use of these Japanese words was, however, incorrect, as some viewers pointed out. Senpai Pusheen wrote:

> As a half [A]sian (Japanese and Vietnamese), I found it very disrespectful to say them incorrectly, nor was it necessary to actually say them. [For example], she could've said "cute" instead of "**かわいいです**" [*kawaii desu*].
>
> Becca Official 2015

Other users were opposed to the entire project of making an English version of "The World Is Mine":

> Another song ruined by America once again. (Christina Organic Enthusiast)
>
> This song was amazing until she made it in ENGLISH!!!!!! (Asuna 5414)
>
> Becca Official 2015

Becca's enacted identity as a fan of Hatsune Miku, as well as of J-pop culture in general, was disclaimed and challenged within fan circles. These criticisms show that some net users and Vocaloid fans did not approve of Becca performing Vocaloid songs due to her "incorrect" use of Japanese. Also, as Christina Organic Enthusiast mentioned, Becca's national and racial identity as non-Japanese certainly made her interpretation of "The World Is Mine" become an object of criticism. The question at stake seems to be how these viewers interpreted her cultural performance, rather than what she wanted to represent through it. Many of them here regarded it as cultural misappropriation or contamination, not as an enacted identity as a fan of J-pop culture.

Users like Mekiko Senpai, who raised the concern over cultural misappropriation of Japanese pop culture, became an object of ridicule on Becca's YouTube channel. Gasping Steven reacted to those who attacked Becca for having done such an inappropriate performance of "The World Is Mine":

> Weaboos complaining about [Becca's] Japanese like they are 100% Japanese.
>
> Becca Official 2015

Weaboos (or weeaboos) refer to non-Japanese who are highly obsessed with Japanese popular culture *and* are willing to "be Japanese." Weaboo is synonymous with "wapanese" and used for both males and females. Someone explained on Becca's YouTube channel:

> A weeaboo is someone who sees Japan as a holy country. They usually disban[d] their own culture, fool themselves into thinking they're Japanese, and end up disrespecting Japan. (Senpai Pusheen)
>
> Becca Official 2015

In contrast with otaku, the word weaboo involves matters of nationality, ethnicity, race, and even an individual's psychological struggle to "become Japanese." Moreover, someone considers it as a derogatory term. In her online article entitled "Am I a Weeaboo? Signs You Might Be a Weeaboo," for example, Christy Kirwan writes:

> If someone calls you a weeaboo, that person is not being nice. If you call another person a weeaboo, don't be surprised if they get angry or take offense. Just like any other insult, don't go casually throwing this word around or you risk making a lot of people mad.
>
> Kirwan 2014

The act of, for example, criticizing others for speaking "incorrect" Japanese tends to be described as part of weaboos' performative acts—in disregard of these users' actual racial and ethnic backgrounds.

Cultural performances are born out of the points where discrete ideas, identities, aesthetics, and realities collide with each other. Anna Tsing (2005) describes such interactive tensions as "friction." Cultures are perpetually co-produced in friction—"the awkward, unequal, unstable, and creative qualities of interconnection across difference" (2005: 4). Friction can also be understood as the "grip of worldly encounter" (Tsing 2005: 1). Friction helps us identify locations where media content circulates globally and how things are connected through the processes. Derivative works of Ryo's Vocaloid compositions emerge from such conflicts between differences in a transnational landscape, whereas the circulation of these secondary works also generates creative, performative, and even collaborative spaces, or front regions, by continually affecting their original meaning and function. As Elin Diamond reminds us, "[t]o study performance is not to focus on completed forms, but to become aware of performance as itself a contested space, where meanings and desires are generated, occluded, and of course multiply interpreted" (1996: 4). Front regions are constantly in a state of construction and reconstruction through transnational flows of media content and frictions occurring in the processes.

In conclusion, Vocaloid fans find diverse ways of constructing identities, sharing knowledge, and circulating interpretations of Vocaloid pieces like Supercell's "Melt" and "The World Is Mine" in multiple, flexible forms. Different types of social media platform help Vocaloid fans circulate derivative works and create front regions. These media platforms and the fans' knowledge, creativity, and individuality come to keep them active and visible. This Vocaloid world also suggests new interpretations of Goffman's classical theory of performance. Performance is not merely an on-stage presentational musical performance,[9] like what we normally watch at popular music concerts today, or a presentation of self in everyday life. But it also functions as a means of learning and knowing, as cultures of circulation, and as causes and consequences of friction between differences. These approaches can broaden our knowledge about different forms of sociocultural performance as processes, practices, and possibilities of becoming. At the same time, these performances detach themselves from the past. A serious scrutiny and conceptualization of fan performance can provide a new dimension in our understanding of popular music fandom today.

Coda

Ryo uploaded his original Vocaloid work "Tsumi no Namae" (The Name of the Sin) onto Niconico two days after the music had been released as a single from Sony on June 8, 2016. This song first appeared in *Hatsune Miku: Project Diva X*, a rhythm game released by Sega Games and Crypton in March 2016 in Japan. Since the release of *Supercell*, Ryo has produced several musical compositions using *Hatsune Miku* software. In addition to "Tsumi no Namae," these compositions include "Kocchimuite Baby" (Look This Way, Baby) released in July 2010; "Sekiranun Graffiti" (Cumulonimbus Graffiti) released in August 2011; and "Odds & Ends" released in August 2012. However, this major label artist did not upload these Vocaloid works onto Niconico. His "Tsumi no Namae" posting was, thus, certainly a surprise to fans. It had been more than seven years since Ryo uploaded his Vocaloid work "When the First Love Ends" onto the site.

"Tsumi no Namae" soon reached the so-called "Vocaloid Hall of Fame," which refers to Vocaloid videos that have gained 100,000+ views on Niconico. Moreover, as of June 23, 2016, the video clip had already received 510,300 views and 522 comments. We can recognize the vitality and connectedness of the Niconico community not only by looking at such quantitative information, but also by being cognizant of the enunciative and textual productivity of these active fans and users. User comments on Niconico include expressions like "welcome back," "welcome home," and "Ryo is back." Ryo's musical works and the distribution infrastructure together provide fans with a way to performatively develop and maintain a sense of belonging to the Niconico community. Viewers leave comments on the video clip, and then new comments are added, making the textual layers thick. Through an act of textual production, Vocaloid fans seem to be collectively constructing a home for both themselves and Ryo, even though Ryo became a major artist in the Japanese popular music industry. Also, since early June 2016, fans have created a number of derivative works of "Tsumi no Namae" in forms of, for example, *utattemita* ("I tried to sing it"), *hiitemita* ("I tried to play it"), and others with their own arrangements and instrumentations, and circulated them through different kinds of online video-sharing platform.

Interactive new media and empowered fan bases combine to engage in the creation processes and circulation of Vocaloid works. What I mean in this book by settings, such as online video-sharing platforms and offline *dōjin* events and conventions, have contributed to the construction of interactive spaces in which users can connect and collaborate with each other and enhance their textual productivity. Meanwhile, it is also important to consider the significance of the synthesizer technology and its technical development, which enabled amateur music-making scenes to continue flourishing across time. The materiality and functionality of the synthesizer technology itself have been constructed historically and socially through continuous interventions of human creativity. The material properties of the technology constitute a malleable and transformable historical subject, which has played crucial roles in expanding our imaginations and made possible the creation of new kinds of musical works that people would never have envisioned some decades ago.

This book has focused more on *context* than *content* to

illustrate cultural and historical backgrounds and the significance of innovations in synthesizer and communication technologies which together led to the creation of the music album *Supercell*—as well as derivative works of *Supercell*. In other words, rather than asking *what* it is, I have illustrated *how* the music album was formed in a broader sense, *how* individuals use it and create something with it, and *how* its surroundings, that is, "media ecology created by and sustaining media convergence" (Nozawa 2016: 178), facilitate these individuals' creative practices. Such surroundings, together with the Vocaloid technology, have contributed to the growth and vitalization—and even sustainability—of DTM culture.

This book can also be considered part of fan studies' continuous attempts to go against mass culture theories, an early model of which was developed by Theodore Adorno ([1938] 1991) with his idea of the culture industry. Adorno views the culture industry's audiences as the "dupes of mass deception" and denies their "relative autonomy of consciousness" (see Bernstein 1991: 18). In this regard, fans become exemplars of passive consumers and "dupes of mass deception" in popular culture. Media scholars like John Fiske (1989) and Henry Jenkins (1992) challenged such mass culture theories by applying the notion of "active audience," developed in cultural studies by the late 1980s.[1] Consumers actively interpret cultural products, texts, and media content, and purposefully use these interpretations in their own sociocultural practices. The concept of participatory culture, then, spotlights the creativity and productivity of fans playing their active roles within a networked culture.[2]

By experiencing a large quantity of derivative works, we may recognize the degree to which individual VocaloPs are enhanced socially and culturally, which indicates these creators' transformative capacity, as a mode of becoming. But at the same time, we also realize the agency of fan discourses in helping to underline the visibility of these Vocaloid works. Fan studies, therefore, provides us with a useful framework through which to understand a fundamental part of media ecosystems in DTM culture. Also, technological and technical aspects of DTM culture play roles in these ecosystems; this book has focused on individuals who have invented and developed Vocaloid technology and software, including Yamaha's Kenmochi Hideki and Crypton's Itō Hiroyuki, among many others. They together constitute the social, thereby contributing to the continuous construction of playgrounds for amateur music-making. The question of how today's DTM culture expands in scale hinges upon such lively collaborations and interconnections, not just between individuals but also among individuals, technologies, and distribution infrastructures. The case of Supercell's *Supercell* in such media ecosystems partly, but essentially, illuminates the dynamic and transformative nature of DTM culture today.

Notes

Introduction

1 By "creator group," I mean a group that consists of composers, lyricists, illustrators, visual artists, and/or designers who together participate in the creation process of cultural works.

2 Vocaloid creators are often called "VocaloPs" (Vocaloid P[roducer]s) in their communities.

3 See also Anthony Giddens (1979, 1993).

4 See Keisuke Yamada (2017).

5 See Matt Hills (2013); and also John Fiske (1992).

6 See Itō et al. (2012).

7 See Sharon Kinsella (1998).

8 See Patrick Galbraith (2012); Itō et al. (2012); Frenchy Lunning (2010, 2011).

Chapter 1: Hatsune Miku and DTM Culture

1 See also Giddens (1979, 1993) for an explanation of the structuration theory.

2 See Fujimoto Ken (2013).

3 Kenmochi was a violinist and belonged to the Kyoto University Symphony Orchestra Ensemble while he was pursuing his master's degree in engineering.

4 See Anne Allison (2006).

5 As a case study, Espen Helgesen's 2015 article, "Miku's Mask," deals with eight- and nine-year-old children in Norway cosplaying the "fictional pop star" Miku.

Chapter 2: How Creative is the "Playground"? Niconico, Piapro, and *Dōjin* Circles

1 See Hiroaki Tamagawa (2012).

2 See, for example, Ōtsuka and Steinberg (2010).

3 In Japanese *netto shakai* ("internet society"), which encompasses the Niconico community, the term "*kami*" (literally translated as "god") has been used to describe someone's outstanding skills in creative activities, including the making of Vocaloid works. See *Nico Nico Pedia* (2016).

Chapter 3: Supercell as a Creator Group

1 See Anne Allison (2013).

2 See Frühstück and Walthall (2011).

3 See Shiba (2013).

4 See Noriko Manabe (2015: 109–49).

5 See Hayarimono Chōsatai (2008).

6 Ibid.

7 See also Anthony Giddens (1993).

8 For the illustration see Huke (2007).

Chapter 4: Supercell's Musical Works and Visibility in Social Media

1 See also Cornel Sandvoss (2005: 29).

2 As Cobachika's gender is unknown, I am using "he" as a matter of convenience.

3 See Akihiro Kitada (2012).

4 "Light novel" is an example of *wasei-eigo*, a Japanese term derived from English words. Light novel refers to a style of Japanese novel, which is short and targeted at young adults. It usually contains anime illustrations.

5 See On'iki data matome site (2016).

6 See Xing Inc. (2016).

7 See singtur (2007).

Chapter 5: Hatsune Miku Fans' Performative Acts

1 See W. David Marx (2012); Carolyn Stevens (2008) for information on the role of talent agencies or *jimusho* in the popular music industry in contemporary Japan.

2 See also Daisuke Okabe (2012).

3 Such "offline" gatherings are often called "off-kai."

4 As lollipop's gender is unknown, I am using "she" as a matter of convenience.

5 This notion spread across the fan communities since Vocaloid producer "Otomania" published a video clip in which Hatsune Miku was holding a leek, while singing "Ievan Polkka," a popular Finnish song. See Yomibitoshirazu (2007).

6 See Dwight Conquergood (2002, 2013) for more information on a performance theory that views performance as a way of knowing.

7 See Michel de Certeau (1984) for the understanding of a practice theory.

8 See Becca Official (2015).

9 See Thomas Turino (2008) for an explanation of the concept of presentational performance, as well as that of participatory performance.

Coda

1 See also David Morley (1986).

2 See, for example, Henry Jenkins (1992, 2006).

References

Adorno, T. W. ([1938] 1991), *The Culture Industry: Selected Essays on Mass Culture*, ed. J. M. Bernstein, New York: Routledge.

Allison, A. (2006), *Millennial Monsters: Japanese Toys and the Global Imagination*, Berkeley: University of California Press.

Allison, A. (2013), *Precarious Japan*, Durham: Duke University Press.

Aoyagi, H. (2000), "Pop Idols and the Asian Identity," in T. J. Craig (ed.), *Japan Pop!: Inside the World of Japanese Popular Culture*, 309–26, New York: M. E. Sharpe.

Aoyagi, H. (2005), *Islands of Eight Million Smiles: Idol Performance and Symbolic Production in Contemporary Japan*, Cambridge, MA: The Harvard University Asia Center.

AV Watch (2011), "Yamaha, utagoe gōsei seinō o takameta *Vocaloid3* o kugatsu hatsubai," *AV Watch*, 8 June. Available online: http://av.watch.impress.co.jp/docs/news/451521.html (accessed 29 October 2016).

Azuma, H. (2009), *Otaku: Japan's Database Animals*, trans. J. E. Abel and S. Kono, Minneapolis: University of Minnesota Press.

BCN Ranking (2007), *BCN Ranking*, 27 September. Available online: http://bcnranking.jp/news/0709/070927_8497.html (accessed 18 July 2016).

Becca Official (2015), "BECCA – 'World Is Mine' MV (English Cover)," *YouTube*, 11 November. Available online: https://www.youtube.com/watch?v=H9qfG30TJsk (accessed 5 June 2016).

Bernstein, J. M. (1991), "Introduction," in J. M. Bernstein (ed.), *The Culture Industry: Selected Essays on Mass Culture*, 1–25, New York: Routledge.

Black, D. (2012), "The Virtual Idol: Producing and Consuming Digital Femininity," in P. W. Galbraith and J. G. Karlin (eds), *Idols* and Celebrity in Japanese Media Culture, 209–28, Basingstoke: Palgrave Macmillan.

Bourdaghs, M. K. (2012), Sayonara Amerika, Sayonara Nippon: A Geopolitical Prehistory of J-Pop, New York: Columbia University Press.

Brasor, P. and T. Masako (1997), "Idol Chatter: The Evolution of J-Pop," Japan Quarterly, 44 (2): 55–65.

Butler, J. (1990), Gender Trouble: Feminism and the Subversion of Identity, New York: Routledge.

Certeau, M. de (1984), The Practice of Everyday Life, trans. S. Rendall, Berkeley: University of California Press.

Cobachika (2012a), "Vocalo kuronikuru daigokai: Melt sonoichi," Vocalo to hito no aida, 26 December. Available online: http://d. hatena.ne.jp/cobachican/20121226 (accessed 11 May 2016).

Cobachika (2012b), "Vocalo kuronikuru dairokkai: Melt sononi," Vocalo to hito no aida, 27 December. Available online: http://d.hatena.ne.jp/cobachican/20121227 (accessed 29 April 2016).

Cobachika (2012c), "Vocalo kuronikuru dainanakai: Melt sonosan," Vocalo to hito no aida, 28 December. Available online: http://d.hatena.ne.jp/cobachican/20121228 (accessed 3 May 2016).

Condry, I. (2009), "Anime Creativity: Characters and Premises in the Quest for Cool Japan," Theory, Culture & Society, 26 (2–3): 139–63.

Condry, I. (2011), "Love Revolution: Anime, Masculinity, and the Future," in S. Frühstück and A. Walthall (eds), Recreating Japanese Men, 262–83, Berkeley: University of California Press.

Condry, I. (2013), The Soul of Anime: Collaborative Creativity and Japan's Media Success Story, Durham: Duke University Press.

Connell, J. and C. Gibson (2003), Sound Tracks: Popular Music, Identity and Place, New York: Routledge.

Conquergood, D. (2002), "Performance Studies: Interventions and Radical Research," The Drama Review, 46 (2): 145–56.

Conquergood, D. (2013), *Cultural Struggles: Performance, Ethnography, Praxis*, ed. E. P. Johnson, Ann Arbor: The University of Michigan Press.

Crawford, G. (2004), *Consuming Sport: Fans, Sport and Culture*, New York: Routledge.

Crawford, G. (2012), *Video Gamers*, New York: Routledge.

Creative Commons (2016), "Attribution-NonCommercial 3.0 Unported," *Creative Commons*. Available online: http://creativecommons.org/licenses/by-nc/3.0/ (accessed 7 April 2016).

Crypton Future Media (2015), "Kyarakutaariyō no gaidorain" [A Guideline for the Usage of Characters], *Piapro*, 16 September. Available online: http://piapro.jp/license/character_guideline (accessed 9 April 2016).

Crypton Future Media (2016), "For Creators," *Piapro*. Available online: http://piapro.net/intl/en_for_creators.html (accessed 20 July 2016).

DeLanda, M. (2002), *Intensive Science and Virtual Philosophy*, New York: Continuum.

Diamond, E. (1996), "Introduction," in E. Diamond (ed.), *Performance and Cultural Politics*, 1–12, New York: Routledge.

Duffett, M. (2013), *Understanding Fandom: An Introduction to the Study of Media Fan Culture*, New York: Bloomsbury.

Duffett, M. (2014), "Introduction," in M. Duffett (ed.), *Popular Music Fandom: Identities, Roles and Practices*, 1–15, New York: Routledge.

Eng, L. (2012), "Anime and Manga Fandom as Networked Culture," in M. Itō, D. Okabe, and I. Tsuji (eds), *Fandom Unbound: Otaku Culture in a Connected World*, 158–78, New Haven: Yale University Press.

Famitsu.com (2008), "Kaihatsusha mo 'mikku miku' ni sareru Vocaloid no miryoku," *Famitsu.com*, 12 September. Available online: http://www.famitsu.com/game/news/1218029_1124.html (accessed 19 July 2016).

Feld, S. (1996), "Pygmy POP: A Genealogy of Schizophonic Mimesis," *Yearbook for Traditional Music*, 28: 1–35.

Feld, S. (2015), "Acoustemology," in D. Novak and M. Sakakeeny (eds), *Keywords in Sound*, 12–21, Durham: Duke University Press.

Fiske, J. (1989), *Reading the Popular*, New York: Routledge.

Fiske, J. (1992), "The Cultural Economy of Fandom," in L. A. Lewis (ed.), *The Adoring Audience: Fan Culture and Popular Media*, 30–49, New York: Routledge.

Frühstück, S. and A. Walthall (2011), "Introduction: Interrogating Men and Masculinities," in S. Frühstück and A. Walthall (eds), *Recreating Japanese Men*, 1–21, Berkeley: University of California Press.

Frühstück, S. and A. Walthall, eds (2011), *Recreating Japanese Men*, Berkeley: University of California Press.

Fujiki, H. (2016), "Networking Citizens through Film Screenings: Cinema and Media in Post-3/11 Social Movements," in P. W. Galbraith and J. G. Karlin (eds), *Media Convergence in Japan*, 60–87, Kinema Club.

Fujimoto, K. (2013), "DTM no rūtsu, 1988-nen ni tōjō shita Myūji-kun no shōgeki" [The Roots of the DTM, the Influence of the "Myūji-kun" in 1988], *Fujimoto Ken's DTM Station*, 22 August. Available online: http://www.dtmstation.com/archives/51868833.html (accessed 13 March 2016).

Fuwafuwa Cinnamon (2007), "Koisuru Voc@loid," *Niconico*, 13 September. Available online: http://www.nicovideo.jp/watch/sm1049371 (accessed 4 May 2016).

Galbraith, P. W. (2012), *Otaku Spaces*, Seattle: Chin Music Press.

Galbraith, P. W. and J. G. Karlin (2012), "Introduction: The Mirror of Idols and Celebrity," in P. W. Galbraith and J. G. Karlin (eds), *Idols and Celebrity in Japanese Media Culture*, 1–32, Basingstoke: Palgrave Macmillan.

Galbraith, P. W. and J. G. Karlin, eds (2012), *Idols and Celebrity in Japanese Media Culture*, Basingstoke: Palgrave Macmillan.

Galbraith, P. W. and J. G. Karlin, eds (2016), *Media Convergence in Japan*, Kinema Club.

Gauntlett, D. (2011), *Making Is Connecting*, Cambridge: Polity Press.

Giddens, A. (1979), *Central Problems in Social Theory: Action, Structure and Contradiction in Social Analysis*, Berkeley: University of California Press.

Giddens, A. (1993), *New Rules of Sociological Method: A Positive Critique of Interpretative Sociologies*, 2nd edn, Cambridge: Polity Press.

Gitelman, L. (2006), *Always Already New: Media, History, and the Data of Culture*, Cambridge, MA: The MIT Press.

Goffman, E. (1959), *The Presentation of Self in Everyday Life*, New York: Anchor Books.

Gotō, M. (2012), "'Hatsune Miku' wa naze chūmokusarete irunoka?" [Why Does "Hatsune Miku" Attract Attention?], *Journal of the Institute of Electrical Engineers of Japan*, 132 (9): 630–3.

Gotō, M., Nakano, T., and Hamasaki, M. (2014), "Hatsune Miku to N-ji sōsaku ni kanren shita ongakujōhōshori-kenkyū: VocaListener to Songrium" [Music Information Processing Research Related to Hatsune Miku and N-th Order Derivative Creation: VocaListener and Songrium], *Journal of Information Processing and Management*, 56 (11): 739–49.

Guitar (2007), "Comic Market 73: Melt sanka kettei!," *Guitars*, 22 December. Available online: http://guitars.jpn.org/?p=729 (accessed 22 April 2016).

Gustavson, L. C. and J. D. Cytrynbaum (2003), "Illuminating Spaces: Relational Spaces, Complicity, and Multisited Ethnography," *Field Methods*, 15 (3): 252–70.

Hamasaki, M., Takeda, H., and Nishimura, T. (2008), "Network Analysis of Massively Collaborative Creation of Multimedia Contents: Case Study of Hatsune Miku Videos on Nico Nico Douga," Proceedings of the 1st International Conference on

Designing Interactive User Experiences for TV and Video, 165–8, Silicon Valley, California, October 22–4.

Hamasaki, M., Takeda, H., and Nishimura, T. (2010), "Dōga kyōdō saito ni okeru daikibo na kyōchōteki sōzōkatsudō no sōhatsu no nettowaaku bunseki: Nico nico dōga ni okeru Hatsune Miku dōga komyunitii o taishō to shite" [A Network Analysis of an Emergent Massively Collaborative Creation on Video-Sharing Website: A Case Study of a Community of Hatsune Miku Movie on Nico Nico Douga], *Jinkōchinō gakkai ronbun-shū*, 25 (1): 157–67.

Haraway, D. J. (2008), *When Species Meet*, Minneapolis: University of Minnesota Press.

Hatsune Miku Channel (2016), "Dansei VocaloP to josei VocaloP," *Hatsune Miku Channel*. Available online: http://www.mikumiku2ch.jp/archives/46373787.html#comments (accessed 4 August 2016).

Hayarimono Chōsatai (2008), "Wadai no netto monsutaa, part 2" [Trendy Net Monsters, Part 2], *Oricon Style*, 5 August. Available online: http://www.oricon.co.jp/trend/hayari/20080805_02.html (accessed 17 April 2016).

Helgesen, E. (2015), "Miku's Mask: Fictional Encounters in Children's Costume Play," *Childhood*, 22 (4): 536–50.

Hills, M. (2002), *Fan Cultures*, New York: Routledge.

Hills, M. (2006), "Not Just Another Powerless Elite?: When Media Fans Become Subcultural Celebrities," in S. Holmes and S. Redmond (eds), *Framing Celebrity: New Directions in Celebrity Culture*, 101–18, New York: Routledge.

Hills, M. (2013), "Fiske's 'Textual Productivity' and Digital Fandom: Web 2.0 Democratization versus Fan Distinction?" *Journal of Audience & Reception Studies*, 10 (1): 130–53.

Huke (2007), "Black Rock Shooter," *Pixiv*, 26 December. Available online: http://www.pixiv.net/member_illust.php?mode=medium&illust_id=279688 (accessed 23 April 2016).

ika (2007), "Miku Miku ni shite ageru," *Niconico*, 20 September. Available online: http://www.nicovideo.jp/watch/sm1097445 (accessed 3 August 2016).

IkaP (2015), "Komike89 ni saakuru sanka shimasu! Vocalo CD tō no hanpubutsu no shōkai" [Our group will participate in Comic Market 89! An introduction of distribution products including VocaloCDs], *Niconico Dōgubako*. Available online: http://niconico-toolbox.blog.jp/archives/1016415918.html (accessed 8 April 2016).

Itō, M. (2012), "'As Long as It's Not *Linkin Park Z*': Popularity, Distinction, and Status in the AMV Subculture," in M. Itō, D. Okabe, and I. Tsuji (eds), *Fandom Unbound: Otaku Culture in a Connected World*, 275–98, New Haven: Yale University Press.

Itō, M., D. Okabe, and I. Tsuji, eds (2012), *Fandom Unbound: Otaku Culture in a Connected World*, New Haven: Yale University Press.

Jenkins, H. (1992), *Textual Poachers: Television Fans & Participatory Culture*, New York: Routledge.

Jenkins, H. (2006), *Convergence Culture: Where Old and New Media Collide*, New York: New York University Press.

Jenkins, H., S. Ford, and J. Green (2013), *Spreadable Media: Creating Value and Meaning in a Networked Culture*, New York: New York University Press.

jospecial (2016), "Talk'n to my baby," *Piapro*, 17 July. Available online: http://piapro.jp/t/Ylum (accessed 21 July 2016).

JP (2015), "Utattemita: 'Melt' (Male Ver.)," *Niconico*, 4 January. Available online: http://www.nicovideo.jp/watch/sm25277015 (accessed 16 May 2016).

Keen, A. (2008), *The Cult of the Amateur*, London: Nicholas Brealey Publishing.

Kelly, W. W. (2004), "Introduction: Locating the Fans," in W. W. Kelly (ed.), *Fanning the Flames: Fans and Consumer Culture in Contemporary Japan*, 1–16, Albany: State University of New York Press.

Kelly, W. W., ed. (2004), *Fanning the Flames: Fans and Consumer Culture in Contemporary Japan*, Albany: State University of New York Press.

Kenmochi, H. (2008), "Kasei gōsei gijyutsu to VOCALOID" [Singing Synthesis: VOCALOID and Its Technologies], *Human Interface*, 10 (2): 161–4.

Kenmochi, H. and Ōshita, H. (2007), "VOCALOID: Commercial Singing Synthesizer Based on Sample Concatenation," Paper presented at the 8th annual meeting for the International Speech Communication Association, Antwerp, Belgium, August 27–31.

Kinsella, S. (1998), "Japanese Subculture in the 1990s: Otaku and the Amateur Manga Movement," *Journal of Japanese Studies*, 24 (2): 289–316.

Kirwan, C. (2014) "Am I a Weeaboo? Signs You Might Be a Weeaboo," *TurboFuture*, 30 December. Available online: https://turbofuture.com/internet/What-Is-a-Weeaboo (accessed 1 July 2016).

Kitada, A. (2012), "Japan's cynical nationalism," in M. Itō, D. Okabe, and I. Tsuji (eds), *Fandom Unbound: Otaku Culture in a Connected World*, 68–84, New Haven: Yale University Press.

Lanier, J. (2010), *You Are Not a Gadget*, New York: Vintage.

Leavitt, A., T. Knight, and A. Yoshiba (2016), "Producing Hatsune Miku: Concerts, Commercialization, and the Politics of Peer Production," in P. W. Galbraith and J. G. Karlin (eds), *Media Convergence in Japan*, 200–29, Kinema Club.

Lee, B. and E. LiPuma (2002), "Cultures of Circulation: The Imaginations of Modernity," *Public Culture*, 14 (1): 191–213.

Lewis, L. A., ed. (1992), *The Adoring Audience: Fan Culture and Popular Media*, London: Routledge.

lollipop (2010), "Ikioidakede negigataraito tsukuttemita," *Niconico*, 15 March. Available online: http://www.nicovideo.jp/watch/sm10034716 (accessed 26 May 2016).

Lunning, F. (2010), "Introduction," *Mechademia 5*: ix–xi.

Lunning, F., ed. (2010), *Mechademia 5: Fanthropologies*, Minneapolis: University of Minnesota Press.

Lunning, F., ed. (2011), *Mechademia 6: User Enhanced*, Minneapolis: University of Minnesota Press.

Manabe, N. (2015), *The Revolution Will Not Be Televised: Protest Music After Fukushima*, Oxford: Oxford University Press.

marasy8 (2009), "'Melt' hiitemita (Piano)," *YouTube*, 4 April. Available online: https://www.youtube.com/watch?v=oySp-jznHQo (accessed 2 June 2016).

Marx, W. D. (2012), "The *Jimusho* System: Understanding the Production Logic of the Japanese Entertainment Industry," in P. W. Galbraith and J. G. Karlin (eds), *Idols and Celebrity in Japanese Media Culture*, 35–55, Basingstoke: Palgrave Macmillan.

Matsue, J. M. (2016), *Focus: Music in Contemporary Japan*, New York: Routledge.

McCarthy, D. (2014), "Labor, Machines, IVR-Enabled Automated Call Centers, and the Design of an Audible Workplace," in S. Gopinath and J. Stanyek (eds), *The Oxford Handbook of Mobile Music Studies, Volume 1*, 135–68, Oxford: Oxford University Press.

Miller, K. (2012), *Playing Along: Digital Games, YouTube, and Virtual Performance*, Oxford: Oxford University Press.

minato (2008), "Ryuusei (Shooting star)," *Niconico*, 13 January. Available online: http://www.nicovideo.jp/watch/sm2019245 (accessed 22 July 2016).

Morley, D. (1986), *Family Television: Cultural Power and Domestic Leisure*, London: Methuen.

Müller, M. (2015), *Fundamentals of Music Processing: Audio, Analysis, Algorithms, Applications*, New York: Springer.

Nico Nico Pedia (2012), "Black Rock Shooter," *Nico Nico Pedia*, 2 December. Available online: http://dic.nicovideo.jp/v/sm3645817 (accessed 7 August 2016).

Nico Nico Pedia (2016), "Kami," *Nico Nico Pedia*. Available online: http://dic.nicovideo.jp/a/神 (accessed 5 April 2016).

NOA (2008), "Melt PV kaitemita (Full Ver.)," *Niconico*, 24 December. Available online: http://www.nicovideo.jp/watch/sm5641312 (accessed 17 August 2016).

Novak, D. (2013), *Japanoise: Music at the Edge of Circulation*, Durham: Duke University Press.

Nozawa, S. (2016), "Ensoulment and Effacement in Japanese Voice Acting," in P. W. Galbraith and J. G. Karlin (eds), *Media Convergence in Japan*, 169–99, Kinema Club.

Okabe, D. (2012), "Cosplay, Learning, and Cultural Practice," in M. Itō, D. Okabe, and I. Tsuji (eds), *Fandom Unbound: Otaku Culture in a Connected World*, 225–48, New Haven: Yale University Press.

On'iki data matome site (2016), "Hatsune Miku," *On'iki data matome site*. Available online: http://karaok.web.fc2.com/artist/hatsune_miku_sakusya.html (accessed 13 August 2016).

Ortner, S. B. (2006), *Anthropology and Social Theory: Culture, Power, and the Acting Subject*, Durham: Duke University Press.

Ōtsuka, E. and M. Steinberg (2010), "World and Variation: The Reproduction and Consumption of Narrative," *Mechademia* 5: 99–116.

Prusa, I. (2012), "Megaspectacle and Celebrity Transgression in Japan: The Sakai Noriko Media Scandal," in P. W. Galbraith and J. G. Karlin (eds), *Idols and Celebrity in Japanese Media Culture*, 56–71, Basingstoke: Palgrave Macmillan.

Ryo (2007a), "Hatsune Miku Sang Sakamoto Maaya's 'Gravity' for Us," *Niconico*, 30 October. Available online: http://www.nicovideo.jp/watch/sm1405937 (accessed 25 March 2016).

Ryo (2007b), "Hatsune Miku Sings Us the Original 'Melt,'" *Niconico*, 7 December. Available online: http://www.nicovideo.jp/watch/sm1715919 (accessed 13 May 2016).

Ryo (2008a), "Hatsune Miku Sings Us the Original 'The World

Is Mine,"" *Niconico*, 31 May. Available online: http://www.
nicovideo.jp/watch/sm3504435 (accessed 13 May 2016).

Ryo (2008b), "Hatsune Miku Sings Us the Original 'Black Rock
Shooter,'" *Niconico*, 13 June. Available online: http://www.
nicovideo.jp/watch/sm3645817.

Ryo (2011), "Interview: Ryo from Supercell," *Anime News Network*,
21 June. Available online: http://www.animenewsnetwork.
com/interview/2011-06-21/interview-ryo-from-supercell
(accessed 27 August 2016).

Ryo (2016), "Hatsune Miku: The Name of [t]he Sin," *Niconico*,
10 June. Available online: http://www.nicovideo.jp/watch/
sm29021785 (accessed 23 June 2016).

Sakuma, H. (2012), "Jinsei hatsu no MIDI ongen – KAWAI saundo
paretto" [The First MIDI Sound Module in My Life: KAWAI
Sound Palette], *Uma Studio*, 3 February. Available online:
http://sakuman390.cocolog-nifty.com/blog/2012/02/midi---
kawai-1-.html (accessed 4 July 2016).

Sandvoss, C. (2005), *Fans: The Mirror of Consumption*, Cambridge:
Polity Press.

Sandvoss, C. (2011), "Fans Online: Affective Media
Consumption and Production in the Age of Convergence,"
in M. Christensen, A. Jansson, and C. Christensen (eds),
*Online Territories: Globalization, Mediated Practice and Social
Space*, 49–74, New York: Peter Lang.

Scott, S. (2008), "Authorized Resistance: Is Fan Production
Frakked?," in T. Potter and C. W. Marshall (eds), *Cylons in
America: Critical Studies in Battlestar Galactica*, 210–23, New
York: Continuum.

Senderista (2016), *Marasy8 Fans*. Available online: http://
marasy8fans.blogspot.com (accessed 2 June 2016).

Sewell, W. H., Jr. (2005), *Logics of History: Social Theory and
Social Transformation*, Chicago: The University of Chicago
Press.

SF2K (2016), "Koremade no DTM no rekishi o yururito

matometemita," *SF2K-LAB*, 4 March. Available online: http://
sf2k-lab.com/dtm-history/ (accessed 15 July 2016).

Shiba, T. (2013), "Boom Boom Satellites x Supercell taidan" [A
Conversation between Boom Boom Satellites and Supercell],
Cinra.net, 15 November. Available online: http://www.cinra.
net/interview/2013/11/15/000000.php (accessed 14 April
2016).

Shiba, T. (2014), *Hatsune Miku wa naze sekai o kaetanoka?*
[Why Did Hatsune Miku Change the World?], Tokyo: Ōta
shuppan.

Shirky, C. (2010), *Cognitive Surplus: Creativity and Generosity in a
Connected Age*, New York: Penguin Press.

Simondon, G. (1980), *On the Mode of Existence of Technical
Objects*, trans. N. Mellamphy, London: University of Western
Ontario.

Simondon, G. (2005), *L'Individuation à la Lumière des Notions de
Forme et d'Information*, Grenoble: Ed. Jérôme Millon.

singtur (2007), "Melt o utattemita (gazeru)," *YouTube*, 12
December. Available online: https://www.youtube.com/
watch?v=WZEvw_WLjDQ (accessed 17 August 2016).

Stevens, C. S. (2008), *Japanese Popular Music: Culture, Authenticity,
and Power*, New York: Routledge.

Sunagi (2009), "Supercell Feat. Hatsune Miku 'Supercell' de
Vocaloid o tadashiku aishitemiru" [I will try to love Vocaloid by
looking at Supercell's *Supercell Featuring Hatsune Miku*], *Yaya
saihate no blog*, 4 March. Available online: http://d.hatena.
ne.jp/sunagi/20090304/1236184508 (accessed 10 August
2016).

Syo (2016), "Miku-chan@FOURTH," *Piapro*, 5 July. Available online:
http://piapro.jp/t/QYLV (accessed 21 July 2016).

Tamagawa, H. (2012), "Comic Market as Space for Self-Expression
in Otaku Culture," in M. Itō, D. Okabe, and I. Tsuji (eds), *Fandom
Unbound: Otaku Culture in a Connected World*, 107–32, New
Haven: Yale University Press.

Tsing, A. L. (2005), *Friction: An Ethnography of Global Connection*, Princeton: Princeton University Press.

Turino, T. (2008), *Music as Social Life: The Politics of Participation*, Chicago: The University of Chicago Press.

ussy (2008), "'Ryūsei' Short Ver de ending-poku shitemita," *Niconico*, 14 January. Available online: http://www.nicovideo.jp/watch/sm2030388 (accessed 22 July 2016).

Wikia (2016), "Melt," *Wikia*. Available online: http://vocaloid.wikia.com/wiki/メルト_(Melt) (accessed 3 May 2016).

Xing Inc. (2016), *Xing Inc.* Available online: http://www.xing.co.jp (accessed 12 August 2016).

Yamada, K. (2017), "Rethinking *Iemoto*: Theorizing Individual Agency in the *Tsugaru Shamisen* Oyama-ryū," *Asian Music*, 48 (1): 28–57.

Yano, C. R. (2002), *Tears of Longing: Nostalgia and the Nation in Japanese Popular Song*, Cambridge, MA: Harvard University Press.

Yano, C. R. (2004), "Letters from the Heart: Negotiating Fan-Star Relationships in Japanese Popular Music," in W. W. Kelly (ed.), *Fanning the Flames: Fans and Consumer Culture in Contemporary Japan*, 41–58, Albany: State University of New York Press.

Yano, C. R. (2013), *Pink Globalization: Hello Kitty's Trek Across the Pacific*, Durham: Duke University Press.

Yomibitoshirazu (2007), "Ievan Polkka @ VOCALOID2 Hatsune Miku," *YouTube*, 7 September. Available online: https://www.youtube.com/watch?v=a5kDclJ9i_A (accessed 28 May 2016).

youhey (2009), "Gasshō Melt-Band Edition- (Male Ver.)," *Niconico*, 17 May. Available online: http://www.nicovideo.jp/watch/sm7068391 (accessed 16 August 2016).

Zaborowski, R. (2016), "Hatsune Miku and Japanese Virtual Idols," in S. Whiteley and S. Rambarran (eds), *The Oxford Handbook of Music and Virtuality*, 111–28, Oxford: Oxford University Press.

Links to Music Videos and Images

Chapter 2

Niconico:

minato, "Ryūsei (Shooting star)," http://www.nicovideo.jp/watch/sm2019245

Ryo, "Gravity," http://www.nicovideo.jp/watch/sm1405937

ussy, "'Ryūsei' Short Ver.," http://www.nicovideo.jp/watch/sm2030388

Piapro:

jospecial, "Talk'n to my baby," http://piapro.jp/t/Ylum

Chapter 3

Niconico:

Ryo, "Gravity," http://www.nicovideo.jp/watch/sm1405937

Ryo, "Melt," http://www.nicovideo.jp/watch/sm1715919

Ryo, "Black Rock Shooter," http://www.nicovideo.jp/watch/sm3645817

Pixiv:

Huke, "Black Rock Shooter" (image), http://www.pixiv.net/member_illust.php?mode=medium&illust_id=279688

Chapter 4

Niconico:

Fuwafuwa Cinnamon, "A Voc@loid in Love," http://www.nicovideo.jp/watch/sm1049371

ika, "Let's All Miku Miku," http://www.nicovideo.jp/watch/sm1097445

JP, "Utattemita: 'Melt' (Male Ver.)," http://www.nicovideo.jp/watch/sm25277015

Ryo, "Melt," http://www.nicovideo.jp/watch/sm1715919

Ryo, "The World Is Mine," http://www.nicovideo.jp/watch/sm3504435

Ryo, "Black Rock Shooter," http://www.nicovideo.jp/watch/sm3645817

youhey, "Gasshō Melt-Band Edition- (Male Ver.)," http://www.nicovideo.jp/watch/sm7068391

Chapter 5

Niconico:

JP, "Utattemita: 'Melt' (Male Ver.)," http://www.nicovideo.jp/watch/sm25277015

YouTube:

marasy8, "'Melt' hiitemita (Piano)," https://www.youtube.com/watch?v=oySp-jznHQo

Rebecca Emily Hollcraft, "BECCA – 'World Is Mine' MV (English Cover)," https://www.youtube.com/watch?v=H9qfG30TJsk

Coda

Niconico:

Ryo, "The Name of the Sin," http://www.nicovideo.jp/watch/sm29021785

Index